YOUR LIFE
YOUR LEGACY

by
Nadia Wong

First Printed in United Kingdom 2020

Published by Conscious Dreams Publishing

Edited by Rhoda Molife and Elise Abram

Typeset by Oksana Kosovan

www.consciousdreamspublishing.com

ISBN: 978-1-913674-26-7

In loving memory of my wonderful, imperfect parents,
Franco Cheung Yau Wong and Maria Teresa Wong (née Ciardiello).

Thank you for bringing me into this world and for giving me the gift of life.
You may not be here in body, but you are very much alive within my soul.
I'll love you for all of eternity.

Acknowledgments

First and foremost, I'd like to thank the parents for being here and doing this work for you and your families, for seeing how valuable this work is, and for taking this journey with me.

I am grateful for my friend and mentor, Emily Jane Harbrecht, who is as passionate as I am about my vision and the work in this book. It is rare for me to have someone that can see life through my eyes and understand my level of passion and enthusiasm for my work. I thank you for being a part of my life; your support has been invaluable.

Thank you to Daniella Blechner at Conscious Dreams Publishing. Your heart-centred company feels like home to me, a safe space where I feel seen, heard, and listened to. I love your passion for and dedication to your work, ensuring the voices of your authors are heard.

Thanks to Elise Abram and Rhoda Molife for accepting my imperfections as a writer and for giving me the freedom to write from my soul. I'm grateful for your guidance through organising all the words that spill from my heart to help make them flow with ease.

Other than my parents, I have to thank my two beautiful sisters, Marisa and Gisella, for allowing me to share our family stories in this book. I sometimes look into your eyes and see mum or dad staring back at me, which reminds me that they still live on inside of us. I love you both with all my soul.

Thanks to my family, immediate and extended – I love every single one of you. Family is everything to me. *You* are everything to me.

A special thank you to Leon and Maia. I am truly grateful that I was blessed to be your mummy, to bring you into this world and be your guide in the first years of your lives. You may not understand the depth of my love right now, but one day, perhaps when you have children of your own, you will. My love for you is infinite, and it has been the greatest honour of my life to be your mother.

"By sharing our imperfections with others,
we are giving them permission
to be perfectly imperfect themselves."
~ Nadia Wong

Contents

"There is no greater agony than bearing an untold story inside you!"
~Maya Angelou

Do you believe that everything happens for a reason? I do. When I was 22-years-old, while I was looking for some paper in my dad's desk drawer, I came across two notepads filled with stories of his youth and life. I was so mesmerised that I couldn't pull myself away as I delved into the very heart of my wonderful yet quiet father. That day changed my life forever, and I finally knew the true meaning of love.

I'd lived with that beautiful human being for 22 years, yet I didn't really know him at all. He became more than just Dad on that day – he became my hero. Looking at life through his eyes and through his experiences gave me a greater understanding of who Dad truly was. I knew him to be a good, hard-working, funny, kind, generous, and loving man, but I'd never seen the vulnerable side of him. I'd only ever known Franco Cheung Yau Wong as my amazing dad, but I'd never considered what he had to endure to make him the man he was.

We have been led to believe that being vulnerable is a weakness, but in my eyes, it is pure strength. Only brave and truly courageous beings can share their imperfections, show their vulnerabilities, and reveal their true souls with others in their time on earth. None of us is perfect or has all the answers to life's questions, but when we open up and share our real selves, we're truly able to feel free, which enables us to connect with others on a much deeper level, especially with our rapidly-growing children.

In no way can I say my father was wrong for being strong for us, but after reading what was in his soul and realising his "humanness", my eyes were opened, and my relationship with him deepened.

His writing and words have been lost over the years, but what was contained within them is firmly imprinted on my heart.

My dad was Chinese, and his words were written in English. He wrote as he spoke, so what he wrote didn't always make sense, but when I shifted my perspective and imagined him talking, everything became clear, which only made it more special. If he had not emptied his heart onto paper, I never would've known the true depth of his beautiful soul.

Almost 30 years have passed since that day. Sadly, my dad is no longer here, but his words will stay with me forever. Little did he know that his memoirs would not only have a profound impact on *my* life, but it will ultimately have an impact on the lives of many through this book.

This book isn't a tribute to my parents alone but a tribute to all parents. It is a journey toward deepening the love and connection within ourselves and our families by writing our own legacies.

You may wonder who I am and why I am here, writing this book. You will come to know me as we journey through this book together, but let me tell you that first and foremost, I am a mother. In addition to being a mother to two teenagers, I am a life coach for parents and kids and an author. My life is about guiding family members of any age through knowing, loving, accepting, and being their true selves, and I do this by creating books and programmes.

After facing and overcoming a mid-life crisis, depression, other life challenges, and turning my life around, I recognised there was a need for more openness in the world. We all face challenges as a part of life, but if we were all a little more open and honest about who we really are and how we feel, we would come to realise that we are not alone.

One could say I had lived a successful life by society's standards because I followed my heart to create the life of my dreams. I had my own successful business at 21, moved to Italy at 32 to start a family and be a full-time mum, and I have lived for years in my happy mummy bubble, growing my own organic veg and spending summer days on the beach. So, how did I end up at 45-years-old with everything I ever wanted, but spending hours crying every day, wishing my life would fast-forward to the end?

We all joke about a mid-life crisis, but when it actually hits, it is very *real* and no joking matter. Due to a series of challenging events in my life, beginning with the death of my dad, I slowly slipped into depression. I had always been a go-getter in life, so this was a new emotion for me. I had had ups and downs, as we all do, but this time, I couldn't find the will to pull myself up, and I fell victim to the darkness and felt powerless over my life and my happiness.

After overcoming my personal challenges, I knew I could not just sit back and watch others suffer. The more I opened up and shared my story, the more people opened up to me about theirs, and I soon realised that I was not alone. Looking at other people's happy lives or seeing their happy faces on social media may make us wonder why we can't be happy, too, but the truth is that we cannot know the emotions behind the smile, and we have no idea how they are truly feeling. There may be pain and suffering in their hearts, or they may be living a life riddled with fear, doubt, and frustration that keeps them awake at night. The deeper I delved into the lives of others, the more they began to share the pain they had buried and their feelings of being completely helpless when it came to their lives, happiness, and emotions. I knew I had to share the lessons I had learned that had such a powerful impact on my life, and I subsequently took the path to become a certified life coach, enabling me to guide others to gain personal power and freedom in their lives.

I now live my life with passion and joy due to an understanding of who I really am, accepting who I am, and most of all, living life as my true self.

My intention for this book and my work presented here is to support you when opening up to who you are at your core and recognising the beauty within you. I am here to guide you through answering 101 questions about your life and experiences, to open your eyes to the gift of your life, and for you to share that gift with your family. Whether you have had a life of joy or struggle, everything through which you have gone has shaped you into the person you are today. My challenges have turned into blessings because they broke me open, and I was able to see all that I had inside. I now know, without a doubt, that I am doing that which I was born to do.

Life is like an ever-changing piece of art. We start off with clean, blank canvasses, and as we grow, we begin to paint the pictures of our lives. We start off carefree and full of colour, but as we progress, we fall, make mistakes, and allow other people to take the brushes, which can feel as if we have no control over how our pieces of art will turn out. What most people don't know is that canvasses can be used time and time again. We can paint whole new pictures over the existing ones and redesign our lives as often as we like. For as long as we live and breathe, the paintings of our lives are never finished, and there is always room for change and improvement. We are here to grow our souls, love, connect deeply with others, and share all that we have and all we are with our loved ones. This is our time. We have only one chance to live life as our true and beautiful selves and to share who we are with our children.

I cannot express how truly grateful I am to have had the opportunity to know the truth and vulnerability of my father through his heartfelt words, as it certainly brought us closer.

In my experience, writing is therapy. It allows us to speak directly from our souls without fear of judgement and without holding back. Only we know who we truly are, and only *we* know the depth of our love, so only *we* can express what *we* have inside of each of us. My father's words had such an incredible impact on my life, and they ultimately led me to where I am today. I learnt about how he experienced life as a child, hungry in times of war. I learnt how, when he was 17, his father died in his arms after being beaten by Japanese soldiers during the invasion of Hong Kong. He talked about how, as the eldest child, it was his duty to step up and take full responsibility to care for his mother and six siblings. He was forced to leave Hong Kong and the girl he loved to find work and earn money for his family. I am overcome with emotion, even as I write this as I will never really comprehend the sacrifices he made over the course of his life for the people he loved.

What I am very clear about, though, is the value of his stories. If he had never written down his thoughts, I never really would have known the depth of his love, strength, and courage. I would never really have known the man I called Dad.

PART ONE

Chapter 1

HOW TO USE THIS BOOK

Before we begin this exciting new journey, I wanted to first congratulate you on making the decision to do this precious work. Whether you are primarily here to heal the pains of the past, find your life's true purpose beyond parenting, or simply to leave your children a loving legacy, know that you are truly amazing. It takes an extraordinary kind of person to understand the value of what you are doing for yourself and your children because it takes courage, dedication, and an abundance of love. Our children, no matter how old, see us as role models. This means we must become the people we want our children to be. It is all very well to tell them they can be and do whatever they want in life if they have dedication, passion, and work hard, but we must walk the walk, not simply talk the talk.

Being here alone and dedicating this time to yourself may be the greatest work you will ever do in your life, so enjoy every step. I promise it will bring your life meaning and purpose. Before we begin, however, here is what I would like you to do as you read this book and write your own life stories:

- Remember that the power and wisdom contained in this book to support your life will not be found in my words but in yours.
- You must walk this road – I am merely here to guide you. If I were your football or tennis coach, you wouldn't expect me to play the game for you to win – you have to play for yourself.
- Relax, enjoy the ride, and do the work with a clear and open heart.

In return, this is what I will do:

- Ask you the right questions to help you open up and share your stories, for these stories can be passed through the generations so your descendants will know the love into which they were born, which will help deepen your family's love and connections.
- Guide you on how to leave words of comfort for your family when they need you so they will feel like you are near when you are gone.
- Help you tidy-up your past and make sense of it to provide you with an opportunity to let go of your past pain and suffering.
- Guide you to understanding yourself on a deeper level and discovering your true purpose.
- Help you to see the beauty of who you are and how much you have to give.

Your words are, perhaps, one of the most precious of gifts you can ever give yourself or your family. When it is your time to leave earth, will you have said all that you wanted to say? Will you be able to leave your children in peace, knowing that you have opened your whole soul to them? What you are doing right here and now is worth so much more than you will ever know. It is worth more than gold or any family inheritance, including photos and memories – it is a little piece of your soul.

Before we begin this life-changing work, it is essential that we go into this with the right frame of heart and mind. So, where do we start? Every worthwhile project in life needs to start with a plan. Unless we know where we are going or what we intend to do, we will likely wander around, hoping that things will somehow get done at some point, but the thing is that we can't leave this important life-work to chance. We need to make it happen.

A plan starts with setting our intentions. This means we have to understand exactly *what* we want to achieve and *why*. Without clear intentions, we will not have the desire to keep going when we don't feel like it.

When we know the value of what we are doing and why we are doing it, we no longer need to push ourselves to complete our wonderful legacies – we are automatically fuelled with love and energy which, in turn, elevates our joy.

So, you may ask, what was *my* intention and my why for writing this particular book? Well, here is my story.

When I was 35, and my first child was a year old, my mum died suddenly – here one day and gone the next, without warning or a loving goodbye. Despite being a fit and healthy person, she just vanished from the earth because a massive aneurysm she had burst. It broke me. I was left shocked, confused, and unable to comprehend where she had gone. I know it sounds cliché, but I felt as if the rug had been pulled out from under my world, leaving me completely disoriented. As a new mother myself, I still needed my mum, but fate had other plans. She was gone without a trace. Our time was up, but I was not ready.

When I was growing up, we had a tumultuous relationship, but in her last few years, we had become really close. We finally saw things eye-to-eye and had become best friends as we spoke openly about our feelings and grew to deeply understand each other. Little did I know that I would only have a few years left with her. I thought I still had time, so I felt cheated and angry when our relationship was cut short. I still had so many questions to ask her, and I still had so much to learn about the beautiful woman that had given me life.

I was so lost without her that it took four years before I could accept that she was gone forever. It was then that I learned a valuable lesson from her sudden death: life has to be lived each day because our time is limited. We all know this truth, but do we live our lives with this in mind? Do we live each day as if it is our last? Do we tell the people we love how much they mean to us? Do we live with whole, open hearts and share the deepest and most vulnerable parts of us to connect more deeply? Do we allow those we love to look deeply into our souls?

We have just one life, one chance, and this is it – right now. None of us knows when our time will come. It could be years from now, but it could be as soon as tomorrow. I'm not saying this to scare you but to remind you of the reality of our mortality. We tend to go through life without giving thought to our inevitable ends, but no matter who we are or how successful we are, the end will come, and that's a fact. Once we accept this as our truth and make peace with it, we will be reminded to live with more joy and carry less of the weight of the past around with us. Here, in this book, in your book, you have an opportunity to see the wonderful life you have led up to this point. You can start taking steps to get to know who you truly are, opening yourself up to more love and joy in the process.

As I think of my parents, I know their words are my most valuable possession, and I hold them inside my heart to comfort and guide me through life's journey. I am able to share them with my children who didn't, unfortunately, get to know my mum and dad. They grew up without grandparents to spoil them with love and hugs – who knows if I'll be around for my grandchildren? Since I truly believe in the gift of our words, I have kept a written record of my life for my children and future grandchildren to which they can turn to when I am no longer here; I have created a legacy.

I believe that every family should have access to their family's history to see into the hearts of those that gave them life. To write is a daunting task for many, so I created a way to guide others through the process. This process eliminates concerns about how and what to write and allows you to focus on the action of putting pen to paper by answering simple questions. I merely provide a path for you, to take you to a deeper understanding of yourself and your reason for being, and to open your life up to more meaning and purpose. Your job here is to step out of your comfort zone and willingly open your heart and soul for yourself and your children, regardless of their age. It won't be easy, but you only have one chance at life, and one opportunity to connect deeply with the people you love most in the world. For them to know you as a soulful being and not only as a parent or grandparent is a priceless gift. By lowering your protective shield to reveal the truest parts of you through speaking from the heart, love will flow more freely.

Throughout this book, I ask a series of questions designed to help you – the author – and your readers see the best parts of who you are and to focus on what is good about your life. Let's begin by strengthening your mindset to ensure this is a wonderful experience. To do this, let's look at five principles for writing your legacy.

- Define your intention.
- Make a powerful promise to fulfil your intention.
- Create a positive mindset (aka getting into "state").
- Write down your why in your introduction.
- Write with joy and light.

Define Your Intention

So, why *are* you here, reading this book and taking on the precious work of recording your legacy? Whatever the reason, you must be fully committed to it. I would like for you to really think about who this is for, and how you feel about writing your legacy. This is history in the making, so you have to be clear on your intention before writing a single word. Your stroll down memory lane might get emotional at times and having a clear intention and a clear vision of the legacy you want to leave will give you the strength and motivation to keep going.

What I am about to say may be hard for some of you to hear; nevertheless, it is a necessary part of setting and defining your intention. We have to face the fact that one day, *we will all die*, so no matter your age, time is of the essence. Although we all know this to be the truth, we do not actually talk about it because none of us knows when our time will come, so it is essential to go through this project with a certain sense of urgency.

Make a Powerful Promise to Fulfil Your Intention

Writing a powerful promise to yourself and your family and displaying it somewhere it can be seen, will remind you of the importance of your intention. It is inevitable that you will get caught up in your daily routine, get distracted, and avoid those things you know are essential to your wellbeing. By writing a powerful promise that connects to your deepest desires as a human being, you will generate fuel and enthusiasm for your mission.

I do what I do as an author and coach because I am passionate about this work, and I have a strong desire to do all I can to lift and support my fellow beings on this journey through life. I *know* that by writing this book, I can help steer you towards your life's purpose and see the value you add to the lives of others. We all matter. Every single one of us is important no matter who we are, how old we are, how educated we may be, or how much we have achieved. It is important to be clear on this, to know your worth, as you make this promise. If you deny your worth, you deny the very love within you, and that is a source of energy for your family. Now, how's that for a life's purpose? I hope you see how writing and reciting your powerful personal promise will fuel you as you write your legacy.

A Sample Powerful Promise

I promise to put my heart and soul into creating this precious gift for my family, to comfort them and remind them of how much they are loved. I understand the value of my life, and the value of my words will allow them to have a piece of my soul with them, always.

I promise to see the best in myself, to share with my children, grandchildren, and future generations to learn who I truly am, deep within my soul.

I promise to write consistently every day and to make this a top priority in my life as my family are of more value to me than anything that might distract me from my purpose.

I promise to love and serve my family by completing this written legacy.

Now, it's your turn. Make it compelling so it touches your very soul and stirs you to action every time you read it.

I promise to _____

_____

_____

_____

Your signature: _____

Date: _____

Create a Positive Mindset

You emit energy, positive or negative, whether you are aware of it or not, so before you begin, it is important to emit positive energy, to be in a positive state of mind. To understand why this is so crucial, consider what happens when you feel negative.

When we are in a negative state, we are not at our best, and we tend to look at the negative aspects of our lives whether they are in the past, present, or future. If we are angry at someone, for example, we look back through our memories concerning that person, focus on what they said or did to upset us, and then focus on how bad we felt. If we imagine the future when we are in that state of mind, we can see only darkness and gloom, so getting into a positive or neutral state of mind in the present moment is crucial as it allows us to see more clearly.

The good thing is that *you* choose your state of mind and the type of energy you emit. How does emitting positive energy help? Well, for one, it helps with those moments when thoughts arise, such as, "I don't feel like writing today." It can also guard against leaving a legacy tainted with negative energy. This is, by no means, meant to imply that you can only write about the joyous moments, but that even when you write about the painful ones, you shine a light on the lessons learnt or the silver lining that comes with the cloud. Being in a positive state of mind when talking to those we love is essential. In life, we can apologise for our wrongdoings or misinterpreted words, but not here. Once we are gone, there is no room to make amends.

Here are a few ideas to help generate positive energy:

- Move your body – you can literally shake off a bad mood. Stand up and wave your arms and legs around until you feel free of negativity.
- Dance to your favourite tune and allow your body to become free of thought.
- Go for a walk in nature and take in the fresh air, even if it is just for a few minutes.
- Look at yourself in the mirror and put on your biggest cheesiest smile. You may feel silly, but the smile will come for real (you may even laugh), and you will feel your spirit instantly rise.
- Read your powerful promise out loud.
- Meditate.

Before I begin to write, whether a book or programme, I sit for a few seconds and ground myself by taking a few deep belly breaths and concentrating on my breathing. As I breathe in and out through my nose, I imagine that I am breathing in good, clean, light energy and breathing out dark, stagnant energy. It connects me to my soul, and I say a little prayer, asking for love and guidance from the universe (which I have written for you a bit later on) to allow my words and feelings to flow freely and easily through me. This may sound a little "cuckoo" to some of you, but it helps me connect with my source of positive energy and opens my heart.

Write Down Your Why

Another way to be fully prepared and ready to write with love and joy is to write your introduction; this is your why. There is a reason for everything we do in life, and this is no different. We eat to nourish our bodies; we sleep to regenerate, recover, and rest; we drive to go wherever we need or want to go; and we talk to communicate and build relationships.

The introduction not only gives your loved ones an insight into why you are writing your legacy for them, but it is also a confirmation of your commitment to yourself to fuel your soul and complete this mission. Once you get started and begin to truly open, you will feel free and joyful as you recount your life's stories. If you are anything like me – and most of you likely are, or you wouldn't be doing this – then you may even shed a tear or two. I get so emotional whenever I write about my family – in a good way – as I feel a true connection to them. If you find yourself crying, it means you are writing from the heart, and it is an indication that you are on track. This is the way I gauge the depth and value of my writing.

Remember to be yourself and not worry about using the right words. Write as if you are speaking to your family so they can get to the very heart of who you are. Listen to your higher-self and remove the mind-chatter. Do what feels right within, not what you think you ought to do. Be authentic and simply write from the heart.

As I said before, my dad's English wasn't great, and at first, when I read his words, I found it hard to understand him. However, when I imagined him talking to me, it all became clear, and it couldn't have been more perfect.

If it had been written in perfect English, it would have still been good, but it would not have been in his actual words. The way it was written was the most beautiful part. It was the very heart of who he was, and of course, I never would have changed that. He was my beautiful, imperfect father.

So, how do you write your introduction? The answer: just as you like. That is the beauty of this project – there is no right or wrong. These guidelines are just that: a guide. All you need to do is write from a place of love and not bitterness and with a spirit of kindness, compassion, and love. This must be a book of joy and love that will heal you and your loved ones in times of need. In doing this, you will also be reminded of all the joy you have had in your life. It is a win for you and a win for them. Everyone will gain from your heartfelt words of love and wisdom.

Here is an example of how you could start:

- *To my wonderful family,*
- *I'm writing this biography for each and every one of you because...*
- *The reason I'm writing this biography is to share my...*
- *One day, I will no longer be here in body, and I wish to leave you my heartfelt words to...*
- *Because of my love for you, I'm leaving a piece of my soul within the pages of this book for you to...*

Write with Joy and Light

"Seek, and you shall find."
~ Matthew 7:7, King James Version

One of life's undeniable, universal truths is that we usually find that for which we are looking. If we look for the reason why life is beautiful with love and gratitude, we will find it. If we look for a reason why life is miserable, we will find that, too. Adversity and loss are a part of growth, but when we keep hold of and focus on difficult experiences, we continue feeding the pain. The thing to do is to accept the hard times, acknowledge their purpose, learn the lessons, and let them go so they will no longer control our happiness. There is no need to be a prisoner to heartbreak and misery.

I suspect the reason many avoid writing their life's story is due to the fear of reliving hard times. The truth is that everything that has happened in the past has shaped who we are today. It is through our troubles and heartaches that we realise our strengths and are reminded of how precious life is.

If others have wronged us or we have made mistakes, they are just that: mistakes. None of us is perfect, and we need to be forgiven our wrongdoings, just as others need our forgiveness. We can use this time and this book to release the grip of the past, forgive ourselves and others, and remind ourselves that we *are* love. We cannot change the past, and we cannot always change our circumstances, but we *can* change how it affects our lives. If we learn from our hard times, we grow into the people we were destined to become. We can grow in love, empathy, kindness, forgiveness, and compassion, just as we can grow in anger, bitterness, resentment, and hate. We do not get to choose our circumstances, but we can 100% choose how we react to them.

So, as you search through the library of your memories and reminisce about past experiences, on what will you focus? The heartache or the lessons learnt? The pain or personal growth? We can make lists of the times that life was tough, but how does feeding bad memories serve us? Remember: this is a book of love and joy. Think about it – if you could have a day with one of your deceased loved ones, would you spend it moaning and complaining, or would you spend every minute with joy and laughter? What would you want for your loved ones after you are gone?

Here is an example:

Even though I was filled with grief and despair of losing ___, the love for my family gave me the strength to get through it...

One secret to writing with joy and light is to be aware. I am sharing the following exercise with you to open your awareness on how you see life. When I first did this experiment over 25 years ago, I was blown away by my results. I carry out this awareness experiment with each of my clients and write about it in every one of my books because it is so powerful. Even if you have done this before, do it again to remind yourself just how significant awareness is to our existence.

1. Wherever you are right now, take a good look around. Make a mental note of everything you see that is brown.

2. After 30 seconds, close your eyes and call out the names of all of the red or blue things you saw.

Please don't read any further without doing this experiment. It will only take a minute, but the effects can last a lifetime and change your perception of life for the better. Do not just take my word for it; it is vital that you experience this for yourself to reap the benefits.

How did you do? How many red or blue things did you see? If you are in a familiar room, then you may have been able to name a few things from memory. Now, take the time to look carefully around, and you will see all of the red and blue objects you missed – in a picture, on a book cover, or in the pattern of a cushion cover, perhaps? As you look around, you will see more and more red and blue – why didn't you see all of this before? It is because you were looking for brown and not red or blue.

This is just how we see life. If you focus on the beauty and all that is right, you will see exactly that. If you focus on your problems and all that is wrong, then that is all you will see, no matter how much beauty surrounds you.

I did this experiment with a client, and she failed to see the big red door right in front of her. Yes, a big red door! It seems crazy, right? But that is what happens when you focus on what is wrong – you may end up missing all of the beautiful things right under your nose. The lesson here is that as you take this journey through memory lane, make sure your eyes are truly open to all that you have for which you are grateful. Be open to all of the colours that brightened your childhood, all of the people who opened your heart, and all of the wins you gained from the not-so-pleasant experiences. As I take you through this book, I will give you some examples of my own life experiences to help make this journey as simple as possible for you.

Enjoy the Process

The secret to living a happy life is living in the present, experiencing and enjoying each and every day, not stuck in the past or worrying about the future, but being fully present now because, quite frankly, we have no idea how many days we have left. We are so used to living in the past or the future that we no longer enjoy the gift of now. As an example of this, when I take my kids to an all-you-can-eat sushi bar, they spend the whole time focused on what they will eat next without taking the time to fully savour what is in front of them. Due to the fear of missing out on what is yet to come, they miss out on the now. Sadly, many of us live in this place every day of our lives, missing out on the joy of this moment. So, immerse yourself in this valuable work and savour every word and every page. As you journey back through your life, you may think that what I am saying is contradictory, but in doing this work, you will come to accept the past as the past, enabling you to leave the baggage of old conditioning that has been weighing you down or holding you back behind. By taking this little trip down memory lane, you will essentially refresh the canvas of your life, giving you a fresh start in the here and now to paint yourself a bright new future.

When writing my first book, I committed to writing at least one page a day, and I would mark a big red cross on my desk calendar to keep me on track. I marvelled at the collection of crosses, which reminded me that each day was a step closer to my goal. If I had not taken small steps one day at a time, I probably wouldn't have completed a book at all, so I implore you to do the same.

Lao Tzu, the great Chinese philosopher, said, "The journey of a thousand miles begins with a single step," and that is what I did. It reminded me that we could do anything we decide to do if we break it down into bite-sized chunks.

This book was designed with this in mind, for you to make time every single day for the next 101 days, and if possible, make a commitment to read and answer one question at a time. When writing my own legacy for my children, I made it a part of my daily routine. Every morning before my kids got up I would sit down and answer a question. I am a morning person, and I do my best work as the sun is rising, but you may prefer a different time of day. You can write for ten minutes or an hour each day, depending on the length and depth of your stories, but through taking one step, one bite, one day at a time, your book will be complete in 101 days.

Whether you decide to write your legacy by hand in your own "My Life, My Legacy" album, or write it out in digital form and print it, every word you write is of value. I wrote out my legacy for my children by hand because it felt right for me. What *is*, however, important is that you write from the heart and without concern about errors or the quality of your writing. We are not here to create a perfect piece of art but to create an expression of your love and devotion.

This is YOUR LIFE and YOUR LEGACY...I am not here to tell you *what* to write but to inspire you to create your own beautiful piece of family history.

PART TWO

A WRITER'S PRAYER

Please grant me the power to write in the pages of this precious book with abounding love and energy to allow my words to flow freely and joyfully from my soul. May your spirit and source of love surround me so my words enter the hearts of all that read them to lift and comfort them in times of need. Bless me with the courage to open up my heart and allow my true soul to shine on the pages of this book to be a glimmer of light and hope for all.
Amen.

In this section, I pose questions to help evoke your most meaningful memories from childhood. Your answers will not only give your children insight into who you are, but they will also help you to understand who you really are and feel gratitude for all that you have. You may end up realising that your glass is, and always has been, half-full.

As you do the work of delving deep within yourself to reconnect with and know your true self, you will come to realise that the hard stuff was essential. Think of the pain and difficulties of the past as lifting heavy weights to build muscles that make you stronger. The old adage "What doesn't kill you makes you stronger", is true, but if you are to live a life of joy, you must stop the self-sabotage of reliving the hard stuff over and over again without also reliving the good stuff; a balance is necessary. So, here we go.

WHAT DID YOU LOVE MOST ABOUT YOUR CHILDHOOD?

Let's begin this journey with a happy memory. When we think back to our childhoods, we usually see glimpses of memories, and we recall the emotions we felt at the time, whether joy, sadness, shame, or pain. This question deliberately asks you to focus on a joyful memory from your childhood. Journeying back isn't about reliving the negative – it is about seeing the past through fresh eyes with gratitude as a focal point. The past was simply what it was and can't be changed, but we can choose to look at the challenges differently, to see them as a part of our personal evolution. As we take this little trip down memory lane, we must consciously seek out the times we were joyful, peaceful, excited, or experiencing any other positive emotion.

I spent most of my life thinking I had an unhappy childhood because I never processed my childhood emotions. Whenever I went back there, I focused on the unhappy times and times when I felt I wasn't loved. It was only when I began to seek out the good memories that I realised they far outweighed the bad. Some of my own happiest memories were spent with our many friends and their families. Our house was always filled with "aunties" and "uncles", close family friends who were like family. My parents were really social, so I grew up surrounded by a lot of kind and loving people. My "aunties" and "uncles" took us out on day trips to the beach or for drives in their cars, which my sisters and I loved because our family didn't have a car. Many happy days were spent eating, laughing, and having fun together.

You may have had a childhood filled with trauma and sadness, or you may hardly have any memories at all, but when you seek out those *happy* memories, you will find them, even in the midst of chaos. We all have ups and downs in life – some more than others – but when you focus on the joyful moments, this is what you will find.

What "labels" were placed on you as a child, and how did they affect your life and belief system?

Regardless of how our parents treated us as children, their ideas and opinions of us became ingrained in our subconscious. When we were told something negative about ourselves, whether it was true or not, we usually believed it. For example, I grew up believing I was ugly because my mum led me to believe that I was ugly. Now, before you shake your head and say what a terrible mother I had, let me explain. Up until I was seven-years-old, I refused to eat real food. There were some foods I would eat, but none were healthy. All I ate were crisps, sweets, and ice-cream, and what child wouldn't want a diet like that? I clearly remember locking myself in the bathroom as soon as I heard the plates and cutlery clattering around in the kitchen. As a result, I was a skinny little thing, the ugly, scrawny one, especially when compared to my beautiful, chubby-cheeked sisters. Though she was worried about me, my mum used to tell me that if I ate, I could be beautiful like my sisters. All she wanted was for me to eat. She was desperate and was only doing her best, but her comments backfired, and I withdrew more. It didn't help that while growing up, I also heard my mum constantly call herself

37

ugly. On top of that, people would say how similar we were, which, in my mind, only confirmed that I was, indeed, ugly.

I carried my ugly label with me right into my mid-forties. It was only when I began to look within myself and do the inner work of healing my past and understanding from where these thoughts had come that I was able to let go of the label. It took a lot of time and effort to rid myself of this limiting belief and label I had chosen to carry. It meant being aware of how I spoke to myself and of my thoughts and turn them around. To do this, I openly apologised to myself, saying, "I'm sorry. You're not ugly, Nadia. You're beautiful." I felt silly to start with, but I persevered, and with time and consistent awareness of my words and thoughts, I was able to free myself from my ugly label.

We all carry various labels with us throughout our lives. Some are self-imposed and others we allow to be imposed upon us, but once we recognise them as untruths and realise there is no hard evidence to back up our thoughts, we are able to let them go. Once we do this, we feel freer and lighter and are able to move forward with greater ease.

What were your mother's best qualities and what did/do you love most about her?

No one is perfect, no matter who they are or how wonderful they may seem to others. Everyone is flawed in some way; however, if we focus on the good, as demonstrated with the colour exercise in Part I, our eyes and hearts will see the good.

I am the mother of two teenagers, so I am currently the tyrant ruining their lives – in their eyes, anyway. Just as many of us blame our parents for everything, our kids will blame us, too, no matter how great we are as parents. As a parent, I know the amount of love, time, and sacrifice I put in for my kids, but they do not see it. I know this to be true because I never appreciated my mum when I was a teen, either. In fact, I only realised how much she loved me and how much patience she had with my sisters and me when I became an adult. It was only when she was gone that I realised just how much she meant to me, and how much patience she had as a mother to three teenage girls while keeping a home and running a family business.

In my heart, I always knew what an amazing human being she was. In fact, she was the biggest-hearted woman I have ever known, and she always thought of others. As a small child, I remember her taking lunch to the elderly ladies living on our street every Sunday. Before she sat down to eat, she would go off with plates in hand to feed the neighbours. I didn't really think much of it at the time – to me she was just my mum who told me off a lot – but as I grew up, I began to understand how unique she really was. She was a wonderful example of love, kindness, and service, and she continued to serve others throughout her life. Whatever she had, she'd share it, even if it left very little for herself.

If like me, you were fortunate enough to have a wonderful role model in your life, it is important to recognise the great gift you had and might still have. If you think your mother fell short in the parenting department, look deeper to seek out her good qualities, and ask if she was doing the best she could under the circumstances. A major part of the work we are doing here is to offer you an opportunity to heal some old wounds and find gratitude in your life. Again, none of us is perfect, and we do make mistakes. Very few parents set out to hurt their children, but sadly, it sometimes happens, and that is when forgiveness is necessary – to free ourselves from the pain of the past.

WHAT RULES DID YOU HAVE TO FOLLOW? HOW DID YOU FEEL ABOUT THOSE RULES? HOW DID THEY HELP TO SHAPE YOU INTO THE PERSON YOU ARE TODAY?

Nobody likes rules, do they? We want the freedom to do what we want when we want, especially as kids. However, research has shown that children raised with clear boundaries feel safer and more loved. There seems to be a fine line between giving children free rein over their lives and their thinking they are not loved because we don't fuss over their every move. Let's be brutally honest here: parenting is hard. We do what we think is right, but according to our children, we always seem to get it wrong. Give them too much freedom, and they think we do not care. Give them too many boundaries, and they think we are too strict. No matter what we do, we will be blamed for how our kids turn out, just as we blamed our parents for our own shortcomings.

Looking back at our parents, we somehow expected them to get it right, but there was no guide book or parenting exam to qualify them for the job. Only through the experience of trial and error, as parents ourselves, do we realise they were doing what they thought was best.

Speaking from my experience, my first child, a boy, was my guinea pig, and all the mistakes I made, I made on him. Poor thing! As a result, I tried not to repeat the same mistakes with my second child. I was over-protective with him and particularly obsessed with him coming into contact with germs. When he refused to touch door handles, I knew I had to change!

Growing up, we didn't have a specific set of rules in place in our household. My mum was very strict, though, especially with me because I didn't eat. I also pushed her buttons more than my sisters. Though I was a little rebel when younger, thankfully, as a teen, I was too scared of her to go too far.

I remember my mum threatening to send my little sister off to a convent to become a nun, not because my sister was bad, but because she didn't want her to turn out like me! I thought it was hilarious, being punished for being too good, but thankfully, for my sister's sake, my mum's threats were empty ones. So, a lot of my childhood memories are that of the conflict between my mum and me. I grew up thinking that I was a bad girl, but when I look back, I was pretty good – I just was not a "yes girl" like my sisters.

There were a few "rules" by which we had to abide, predominantly good manners and kindness towards others. For example, when on a bus, we had to give up our seats to adults, which is something I still do now. In fact, while sitting on an airport bus taking us from the plane to the terminal recently, I looked around to see if any elderly people needed my seat only to realise that I was one of the oldest there. On that occasion, my thoughtfulness backfired to slap me in the face. Thanks, Mum!

We were also taught to be respectful to adults, and of course, say "please" and "thank you" at any given opportunity. These are the same "rules" by which my children abide because I believe that simple kindness and respect for others is important in life.

WHAT DID YOU DO THAT GOT YOU INTO TROUBLE AS A CHILD, AND WHY DO YOU THINK YOUR PARENTS REACTED THE WAY THEY DID CONCERNING YOUR BEHAVIOUR?

As children, most of us misbehaved at some point, but it wasn't because we were bad – we were simply dealing with our emotions in the only way we knew how. Even now, as adults and parents, most of us are still emotionally fragile at times and struggle with our emotions, so how are children supposed to manage theirs?

I was a highly sensitive child, and my parents saw me as "badly behaved", but it wasn't that I was a bad child – I simply needed extra emotional support.

It took me almost 50 years to understand the emotions carried with me from childhood. I spent my life looking for answers to life's big questions, essentially seeking my true self, but at the core, I was still a little girl who believed I was not good enough. Once that little girl was brave enough to stand up to face her demons, they no longer had a hold on her.

I believe that most of life's challenges come from not knowing who we are. Labels are placed on us from birth by our well-meaning parents as they tried to shape us into the people they wanted us to be to give us the best chances in life, but in doing so, they unwittingly stifled our true selves. Generally, we learned that if we want to be accepted and loved by others, we had to behave a certain way, and essentially, not be ourselves. Despite this, at times, our free spirits couldn't contain themselves, and we were consequently labelled accordingly, never really getting to know our true selves. This also applies to our parents, our grandparents, and all the generations before them. They, too, were labelled and conditioned into believing who they were and reacted to life according to the same misconceptions, passing on the patterns of the past. If *we* don't break that pattern, all of our past conditioning will continue to be passed down through our future lineage. This is why it is important to take the time to understand that we are not who we "*think*" we are due to what we have been told. We decide who we are and who we want to become.

In doing my own work, I came to the realisation that I was jealous of my sisters and my mother's affection for them. My little sister was born only 11 months after me, so I most likely didn't get the attention I wanted or needed at the time, which is why I behaved the way I did. As a highly sensitive child with a lack of emotional intelligence, I lashed out, and my poor mum probably didn't know how to handle me. I grew up believing she didn't really love me – well, not as much as my sisters, anyway – but it wasn't the truth. With everything else on her plate, she simply did her best.

I share my personal stories to encourage you to seek a deeper understanding of yourself and the relationship you had with your parents. As well as exploring your emotions, put yourself in their shoes to really connect with them and understand their reactions and behaviour. You may have been brought up to put on a brave face or encouraged not to be open about your feelings, but there is nothing more courageous than opening your heart and sharing the deep emotions within.

By opening up and *being* who we truly are instead of brushing off our emotions – or worse still, burying them – we inspire others to do the same, encouraging deeper connections.

WHAT WERE YOU GOOD AT, AND WHAT WERE YOU PRAISED FOR AS A CHILD?

The funny thing about life is that we never forget our challenges and shortcomings, but when it comes to our wins, we often struggle to acknowledge them. When asked questions focused on the best parts of who we are, we find them harder to answer. Why is this? It is probably due to our old thought patterns from deep-rooted conditioning that well-meaning others expressed through statements like "Don't be a showoff," "Who does she think she is?" "Who do you think you are?" "What makes you so special?" These are some of the things we grew up worrying people might say about us or to us. Blowing one's own trumpet is often frowned upon and seen as boastful and proud. Pride is and was, in fact, widely known among Christians as one of the seven deadly sins.

Of course, it is healthy – and some might say essential – to have a sense of pride and self-respect, to recognise your gifts and talents and share them with the world. Pride, as a sin, is thinking that you are better than others. Acknowledging your unique skills and talents and sharing them is simply about knowing your worth, value, and purpose. Regardless of who we are and how we are valued by ourselves and others, we are all of equal worth as human beings.

As you answer this question, think about what made *you* proud of being you. Perhaps it was the time you sang in a school concert, danced in a school ballet, played exceptionally well in a football match, made people laugh, wrote a story, painted a picture that your teacher chose to put up on the class wall for parents' evening, or the way you treated a friend who was sad. Don't be too concerned about whether you were recognised for this talent or not. The important thing is that what you did made you feel good, meeting your standard of achievement.

When I answered this question, I learnt that I was my biggest critic. I was also a self-saboteur, believing I didn't have much to offer the world. I told myself that my time had passed and all I could do now was to teach my kids to use their talents to make a difference in the world but wasn't I being hypocritical by not doing the same? The deeper I searched within myself, the more I realised that I had unused potential. I wondered how I might feel if I were to look upon my children as adults to see them living as I was. Would I be happy that they had sold themselves short? It was then I realised it was my job to be an example for them and not just acknowledge but live out my talents, and I couldn't have done that without honestly answering the question above.

HOW WERE YOU REWARDED FOR GOOD BEHAVIOUR AND ANY OTHER ACHIEVEMENTS?

This book actually started as a programme based on 101 questions I created to provide a simple way for parents to leave their children more than just memories. Despite the fact that I was almost 50-years-old, I still felt like I needed my mum and dad in my life, so I paved the way for others to have what I desperately wanted.

Once my programme was complete, I tested it by writing my own legacy based on my answers. Even though I had created the questions, this was a tough one for me to answer as I honestly could not remember being rewarded for good behaviour, but I had to follow the programme – and my own advice – and dig deeper to find an answer. It had to be in there somewhere. Sure enough, I found the memories that brought a smile to my face, and I hope you find yours, too.

The truth is that we were probably praised countless times by our parents and teachers, but we remember the reprimands clearer. What we felt were unkind words or put-downs seemed to cut through our skin to our core, but do we remember being praised for taking our first steps, eating our peas, making our bed, or winning a race? Do our children remember all the love, praise, and devotion we shower on them? When I asked my children this very question, they struggled to think of a time they had received praise, even though I praise them regularly, yet when I asked them about being reprimanded, they immediately remembered every time.

The other thing to remember is that a reward can come in different forms. When I was six- or seven-years-old, we were on holiday in Scotland. One day when out for lunch, I not only ate a whole bowl of rice but asked for more, and my mum literally burst into tears. I'd never seen her so happy with me. I am bubbling away as I write this as I can still see the look of joy on her face. That joy, her joy, was a reward for me. I clearly remember how happy I felt to have made her so happy, simply by eating. From that moment on, I ate better and more regularly. Even though my mum and I still had our moments, I felt more loved.

I urge you to rise to the challenge of answering these tough questions. Open your heart and mind to see seemingly mundane events as bright moments. The more I looked for times I made my mum smile, the more I found, so take your time thinking about each question and let the happy times flow back to mind. Challenge your perspective to find the joyous moments that have always been there.

WHAT ARE YOUR HAPPIEST CHILDHOOD MEMORIES?

For me, these moments are small and seemingly insignificant, but they were the ones when I felt loved. For example, I remember sitting on my mum's knee as a small child when I wasn't feeling well. We were on holiday in Italy at my nonna's at the time. My sisters were outside playing, but because I couldn't go out, my mum sat me on her knee and simply cuddled me. I clearly remember how I felt, where I was, and my surroundings. I had her full and undivided attention, and I lapped up every second of it. For me, at that moment, feeling poorly was worth it as I had my mum all to myself. As she was always busy working, taking care of the family and house, cooking, and serving whoever needed her help, these one-to-one moments were rare, and I felt very special.

In Marie Kondo's book, *The Life-Changing Magic of Tidying Up*, a guide to effective decluttering, the author tells us to empty the contents of the cupboards and drawers into the centre of any room so we can clearly see what we have. The next step is to work through the contents, deciding which items bring us joy. Those that don't are let go, leaving space to keep those that do. Think of the work you are doing with this book as the same process, one of tidying up your memories and thought patterns. No one else can sort through your wardrobe to decide what you like and want to keep, and nobody else can truly sort out your emotions to decide what means something to you and what does not. You can get a stylist or a therapist to help, but ultimately, you must do the work yourself.

Your values and beliefs about yourself, though unique to you, are largely based on what you were raised to believe. The process of asking yourself questions like the ones above to journey back through your childhood should help you sift through your beliefs to choose what is worth keeping and what needs to be discarded, what serves you and what is holding you back. In doing so, you leave space not only to fully enjoy meaningful memories but also to create new and exciting ones that will ignite your inner light.

As you recount your happiest childhood memories, pay close attention to how you feel, what goes through your mind, and why these moments are so special and memorable. Remember: the fact that you can recall these memories means they were significant for you, so as you write, open your heart and empty out its contents so your family will know and understand you on a much deeper level. If you are not used to opening up, this may be difficult to begin with, but the more you do it, the easier it will become. Just like all new skills, it takes persistent practise and perhaps a little blood, sweat, and tears, but you know as well as I that your family is worth it.

HOW DID YOU CELEBRATE YOUR BIRTHDAYS GROWING UP, AND HOW DID THAT SHAPE YOUR ATTITUDE IN LIFE?

I loved birthdays as a child because every year, my mum would make "*struffoli*", my favourite honey balls covered in rainbow-coloured "hundreds and thousands". In fact, my mum was famous amongst our friends for throwing the best birthday parties with music, party games, great food, and a lot of friends. She loved entertaining, and our parties were simply the best. However, as I grew up and grew out of kids' birthday parties, my birthdays were never the same.

I hated my birthday for most of my adult life, but I didn't really understand why. I became anxious for a couple of weeks before the dreaded day, thinking perhaps it was fear of ageing, but as soon as it passed, I was fine again, which made no sense. I began going on holidays or taking short breaks to "celebrate" my birthdays, which made it easier to deal with them. Once I started doing this inner-work, the truth about the anxiety concerning my birthday came to light, and I recognised the negative mindset pattern I had created. I was not running off to celebrate; I was running away to hide, and it stemmed from one bad birthday experience – my 21st.

Because it fell mid-week, I decided to have a huge dinner party so my guests would not have to worry about it being a late, drunken night. I invited 100 people to a local hotel I had booked with a full, hot buffet. I even designed my own dress and had it handmade for the occasion, but little did I know, all my time, money, and energy would be wasted because only 20 people came, even though 80 had confirmed.

This was a traumatic experience for me, and it made me value myself less. I came up with all manner of stories to justify what had happened: nobody cared about me; no one liked me; I was not nice enough or good enough. Was I worth nothing? I never considered that people might have simply changed their minds, which had nothing to do with me. Maybe mid-week was just not as convenient as they'd initially thought, especially after a long, hard day's work. Nevertheless, I was hurt. Why am I telling you this? Because I let that one experience change my whole perspective, and apart from my wedding, it was the last party I ever had.

Even though marriage was a part of my life's plan as I hoped to start a family, I really didn't want a wedding, but my mum and husband did, so I let them talk me into it. I agreed, but I let them organise the wedding they wanted. I wasn't interested in the details, and I didn't even want a wedding dress, but my mum insisted on buying me one, and in all honesty, I was happy to quietly tie the knot and go for pizza with family and friends afterwards.

Even though I didn't quite realise it at the time, I was allowing my past experiences to shape my future. Instead of making a clear and conscious decision based on present circumstances, I was reacting subconsciously to a past traumatic event. There was no real reason why I should have denied my husband a wedding or my mum the experience of seeing her daughter get married, and I had to get over my misguided perception to break the pattern.

We cannot change our experiences, but we can acknowledge them, decide whether to allow them to gauge our worth, and accept them as life's lessons.

If we don't make peace with unpleasant experiences, we can carry the associated unpleasant feelings with us without being aware of how limiting they can be, but once we recognise and break old thought patterns, we can change our way of thinking and make more conscious choices in the future.

How did you celebrate special occasions with your family? What was the best gift you were ever given?

When I asked my 13-year-old daughter what she loved most about Christmas, she said it was our family's Christmas tradition. This surprised me, but it also put a smile on my face as I honestly thought she would say the gifts. As parents, though we do our best for our children, it is always special when they genuinely value what we do.

If you did celebrate Christmas, for example, and remember how excited you were waking up on Christmas morning to gifts under the tree, you probably passed the same tradition on to your children for them to experience the same excitement and anticipation. As you look back at your childhood, you'll be reminded of how important family and family traditions are.

One of my favourite memories is of my dad telling the story of our family's Christmas miracle, and I never grew tired of hearing it.

Like a lot of families, there were times when resources were in short supply. My dad worked as a chef in a hotel, and my mum worked from home as a dressmaker for a local factory. Due to having three girls under five-years-old, my mum had her hands full during the day, so she had to work through the night to earn enough money to help pay the bills, but one year, things were particularly difficult. It was a few days before Christmas, and my parents were really upset because, despite all the extra work they had put in, they still had no extra money to buy food or gifts. I remember dad saying, "I only had enough money to buy my bus ticket to get me back and forth to work, but I decided that I'd walk the long distance to work and gamble my last 50 pence on the horses. It wasn't enough money to give us Christmas, but I decided to take my chances." He knew it was a longshot, but he prayed for a miracle, and his prayer was answered. He said that to see my mum's face light up when he walked through the front door, his arms full of food and Christmas gifts for us all was one of the happiest moments of his life. Even as I write now, I can still see the beaming smile across my dad's face as he told his story.

I love everything about Christmas as it evokes all of the happy memories of joy and excitement in my family's life, past and present. With so much love and joy in the air, it is a magical time for me, with or without the gifts.

The reason we love giving gifts so much is that we love the feeling we get from making someone else smile and feel valued and loved. When we receive gifts, we also feel valued and loved by others. Gift-giving isn't about the gift itself but an exchange of love and value, giving us a sense of worth.

In my experience, when I have received the gifts for which I had hoped, I felt loved and understood, but when I did not, I falsely believed that the opposite was true due to my old conditioning and lack of self-worth. I didn't consider other possible factors, such as a lack of funds, time, or imagination. Due to the term, "treat others as you wish to be treated", it is only natural for us to give gifts we would like to receive, but that thought did not even cross my mind.

When you think back to the times you received certain gifts, pay close attention to how you remembered feeling, and with your adult mind, you may realise you associated that gift with an old thought pattern that may or may not have been a happy memory. The thing we must always remember is that the greatest gift we can give and receive in life is the gift of love and time.

WHAT HOUSEHOLD CHORES DID YOU DO GROWING UP? WHAT DID YOU LEARN FROM HAVING THIS RESPONSIBILITY?

You may wonder why I ask such a question, but it is an essential one to help us understand how our upbringing shaped our thinking where work is concerned. When speaking to others about their lives, I began to see a pattern emerging concerning this matter. Those that worked as children to play their part in the upkeep of the family and home seem to be more content in life. Those who were "spoiled" and were not given any responsibilities found life tougher than expected because they were unaccustomed to life in the real world.

Let's look at the meaning of the word "spoil" for a moment. The first definition in the *Collins English Dictionary* is "to damage (something), with regard to its value". If that is the meaning, why is it that children are jealous of spoiled kids? I can only speak for myself here, but I felt that spoiled kids were more loved than I was. They seemed to get everything they wanted, they didn't have to do chores or work for what they wanted like me, so why were they called spoiled? It baffled me as a child because I couldn't see anything wrong with being spoiled, but as I grew up, I started to appreciate the gift my parents had given me: the gift of developing a good work ethic instead of spoiling me.

I remember standing, ironing, and looking out of the window, watching my friends play, silently cursing my mum for making me do housework. In my eyes, she was a tyrant, and I was being punished by having to do her dirty work. Funny, isn't it? Now, as I watch my children iron their own clothes, I smile as I think of what might be going through their minds. Mind you, I don't force my kids to iron or have battles with them over it – I simply do not iron their clothes. Either they can go out looking untidy, wearing wrinkly clothes, or they can iron.

As you think about your own upbringing, consider what your parents' intentions were and the reasons behind their parenting decisions. If you were one of the lucky "spoiled" kids, perhaps your parents were trying to protect your childhood by giving you the best childhood experience they could. If you were forced to work for all you had, think about the benefits gained from your experience. Of course, there are always exceptions and extremes, but for the majority of us, it is important for us to remember that regardless of how we were treated, there were probably good intentions and love behind our parents' actions.

WHAT WERE THE MOST VALUABLE LESSONS YOU
LEARNT FROM YOUR MOTHER?

I learnt so much from my mum – her successes and her mistakes – and I've used those lessons to shape myself into the mother I want to be for my children. Even though my mum was not openly loving and affectionate with us when we were younger, she softened as she got older. I recognise the deep love she had for me and my sisters, which she demonstrated in her own unique way. She simply spoke a different language of love from me, which I didn't understand at the time, but I am truly grateful that we ultimately connected profoundly.

Because my mum was the oldest girl in her family in Italy, it was her duty, as a female, to take care of the family home and six siblings alongside her mum. Her youngest brother, Geppino, was 15 years younger than her, so she became his second mum and sadly, didn't have the opportunity to have a real childhood. Due to her role as a female in Italian culture, she knew she didn't want to spend her life running after men to please them, so left Italy in her early twenties. She taught my sisters and me to be strong, independent, hard-working, free-thinking women. The only bit of advice she ever gave us concerning relationships was "Don't marry Italian men," as she didn't want us to get sucked into the male-dominated culture, but guess what? All three of us married Italian men!

I used to believe that my mum didn't talk openly about her struggles and insecurities, but the more I delved into understanding my own deep-rooted conditioning and my relationship with her, memories of her telling stories about her life came to light. She may not have spoken openly about her emotions, but she did teach us many lessons about life. The truth is that I probably wasn't paying that much attention to what she was saying as it simply wasn't that interesting to me then. If only I could go back, I'd absorb every word.

I learnt about gratitude through my mum as she recounted stories of growing up during the war with only dandelion leaves and flowers to eat at times, and about her and her siblings running out excitedly to meet the person who brought flour so they could make bread and eat something more substantial. Through her stories, she taught me that in the midst of darkness, there is still joy to be found in the simple and seemingly insignificant things in life like bread.

I have always taken time to talk with my children about all aspects of life, including love, relationships, and their dreams and aspirations; however, the older they got, the more disinterested they became, saying, "Do we have to talk about this stuff again?" I would have loved to have these deep and meaningful conversations with my mum; instead, I do it with my children as an expression of my love, but my kids' reactions are reminders that love has so many faces.

Parents are not the only teachers in our families as our children are our greatest teachers, and I have learnt many lessons from mine.

My mum may not have been physically affectionate with me as a small child, but because I was openly loving and affectionate with her, she changed over the years. That is not to say that she was wrong, and I was right; we simply loved differently.

We are all doing our best to be the best parents we can be. We have undoubtedly made mistakes and needed to learn as we grew, but through empathy, understanding, and forgiveness towards ourselves and others, we can release the grip of the past, giving us the freedom to keep moving forward with love.

What personality traits do you believe you inherited from your mother, and why do you believe this to be true?

Can we inherit personality? The word, persona, originates from a Latin word that means "theatrical mask" – does this imply that personality is inherited or is it acquired? I have no evidence for this, but I do believe that we can pass down our values through our words, actions, and behaviours, whether positive or negative, and this has an impact on our personalities. Small children can learn two or three languages without effort, simply by listening to their parents communicating in those languages – imagine what else they can learn.

I also believe that we subconsciously pass on our energy. If we are born into caring and loving families, for example, the chances are that we will be inclined towards being caring and loving, too. The same goes for those who were born into families that are, perhaps, unloving, racist, or prejudiced against other religions, for example.

We were all born as pure and perfect beings, but as we grow, we absorb the energy around us, which, in turn, shapes our personalities. Whether we inherit our parents' negative energy of anger and prejudice or positive energy of love and kindness, we ultimately choose who we want to be.

For me, understanding that none of us is born evil allows me to be more open-minded, compassionate, and forgiving towards others. The old saying, "Before you judge a man, walk a mile in his shoes," reminds me that we cannot judge others as we do not know who they are or what values or energies they might have "inherited". In fact, we would each have to have walked in a man's shoes for a lifetime to truly know what is going on in his heart and mind.

Something I believe my mum passed on to me is her concern for other's wellbeing. She would never have walked past someone in need, knowing she could have done something to help. It was simply her nature, and if she couldn't help, she'd struggle to hold back the tears. Her love, empathy, and compassion for others were incomparable, but I like to believe I "inherited" a little piece of it. This is one of the reasons I do this work – I feel a calling to serve, like a pull of my heartstrings to ease the suffering in the world wherever I can. Have I inherited this from my mum, or did her acts of loving-kindness towards others shape me? I don't know, but I feel the same energy of compassion that I grew up with.

HOW DID YOUR MOTHER INFLUENCE YOUR LIFE FOR THE BETTER?

We all influence the people within our reach whether or not we choose to do so with our actions and behaviours, but the question we have to ask as parents is: *Are we influencing our children for the better?* None of us is perfect, and we all make mistakes. We all make bad choices and fall from time to time, which is completely natural and even expected, but it is what we do after this happens that has the biggest impact on our children. If they witness us picking ourselves up and brushing ourselves off, they will naturally follow suit. We are their role models, and they will grow up using our behaviours as guides to becoming adults. This inner work is not easy as we have to face the truths behind who we are. We even have to face our feelings of guilt, perhaps because we are not the best influences in our kids' lives; however, it is never too late to start. We all have ups and downs at different ages and different stages on our journeys. We experience periods of joyful flow and times of treading water, barely able to keep afloat, but again, it is how we react to life that influences our children. We cannot protect them from life forever because, sooner or later, they will come face-to-face with the real world and real challenges unprepared. What we *can* do is show them by example.

Growing up, I had no idea of the wonderful influence my mum had on my life because she simply was who she was. I loved her because she was my mum, but I didn't appreciate her, and if I am honest, I didn't even like her at times. By taking a journey through my past, I can now see there was a lack of connection between the two of us, but sadly, we didn't have the knowledge or understanding about emotional intelligence at the time that might have helped us to build that deep connection. My mum simply didn't know what she didn't know. As a mother, I can look back and see all the things my mum did and said that had a positive impact on my life. Referring back to the colour experiment we did at the beginning of the book, as a child, I wasn't focused on all the wonderful parts of my mum. Even though there were many, I could not really see them.

Looking at my mum's life now and the influence she had on me through being herself, I am in awe of her. At 22-years-old, she left the safety of her family in Italy to escape a life she knew she didn't want to live and moved to the UK without speaking a word of English. A factory in Norwich was hiring Italian dressmakers, so she and a couple of girls from her area went off on an adventure. Her mum was so angry with her for abandoning her family, but my mum's strong will and desire for a better life would not let anything or anyone stop her. She had a great life, great friends, and loved life until she was ready to settle down and get married. It was then she met my dad, a kind and gorgeous Chinese gentleman, who stole her heart. Just imagine the scandal when she told her parents! She was not only the black sheep of the family because she had left the flock to live a life she wanted, but she was also going to marry a Chinese man!

My mum was an example of a strong, kind, and beautiful woman, living a free life and never letting other people influence her choices, and I couldn't have had a greater influence for good in my life.

WHAT WERE YOUR FATHER'S BEST QUALITIES, AND WHAT DO/DID YOU LOVE MOST ABOUT HIM?

It is so important that I ask you these questions in a way that allows you to focus on the positive aspects of your life, to see things you have not seen before. I could ask you to describe your father, but your answer will depend upon your present state of mind. Instead, I am asking you to intentionally list the good qualities, forcing you to find them. That is not to say that your father had no negative qualities, as we all do, even if we don't always like to admit it.

If the love between a parent and child is unconditional, then we love each other regardless of how well we get on or how we treat each other. Fundamentally, all love is unconditional because if it is not, is it even love? Is love real if we have to act or behave in a certain way to be accepted and loved for who we really are? Do we have to be the perfect children or parents to be loved?

If our parents did not always treat us or love us the way we wanted, these questions might touch a nerve, but ultimately, we do not know what emotional baggage they had to carry in life. We can simply choose to love them unconditionally or not.

My dad was a wonderful example of a gentleman. He was a gentle man – kind, thoughtful, generous, and hard-working – but most of all, he was present in our lives, and that was what I valued the most; I never once doubted his love for me. Even though he didn't open up and talk about his emotional past, he would openly tell us how much he loved us and shower us with affection.

He was also funny and playful, and he had the biggest heart. I can see why Mum fell in love with him. I have yet to meet anyone who didn't love my dad. Even when my Italian grandparents met him on the day of my parents' wedding, they instantly fell in love with him.

My parents were equal partners. They shared everything, especially the workload. As well as being a hands-on father, he would cook, clean, vacuum, and do the ironing, and I never once heard him complain.

Maybe I shouldn't admit this, but as a child, I loved my dad more than I loved my mum because he was so much softer and kinder and rarely said no. As a mother, I have so much more respect for my mum and realise that as the disciplinarian in our home, she was actually a more effective parent than my dad! Due to a good balance of love and discipline in our home, the "good cop/bad cop" seemed to work because both my sisters and I turned out pretty well if I do say so myself.

What valuable lessons did your father teach you?

We weren't all blessed with a kind and loving father to guide us through life, but whether we had a fully present father or an absent one, we learned valuable lessons from them. One thing I will ask you to remember is that most of us are doing the best we can with our level of knowledge, understanding, and consciousness. We may not have had the perfect father or mother, but perhaps they didn't either, and they didn't know any better – if they had, they probably would've done better.

As parents, we try to teach our children the lessons we learnt in an attempt to protect them from making the same mistakes as us. It does not always work though, because they, too, had to learn "the hard way". Everyone experiences pain of some kind, whether it is heartbreak, health problems, emotional trauma, or feelings of unworthiness and loneliness, and so will our children. They must have these experiences to learn, grow, and evolve.

My dad was forced to step up at a really young age to take charge of his family after his father died. That could not have been easy for him, but I believe it made him a better man and a wonderful father. He did not sit me down and give me specific life lessons, but rather, taught by example. He taught me the value of family connections, and through writing his memoirs, he taught me the value of leaving the legacy of my words for my children. My dad was a kind, thoughtful, and loving man with a passion for food. He loved cooking for his clients in his restaurant, and he went joyfully to work every day, sharing his love and passion with the world. It did not make him rich by worldly standards, but it made him rich in so many other ways as it made him happy. I never once heard him complain about work. He was grateful that he was able to live each day doing what he loved with an open and loving heart.

Even on his deathbed, at 78-years-old, he asked us to organise a huge Chinese buffet for guests at his wake as he wanted to make sure everyone would be fed well. He was dying, yet he was still thinking of his guests, ensuring they would be looked after.

That, in my eyes, says it all. What greater life lesson could he have taught me?

What personality traits do you believe you inherited from your father, and why do you believe this to be true?

According to the *Cambridge Dictionary*, the saying, "The apple doesn't fall far from the tree" means that "a child usually has a similar character or similar qualities to his or her parents", but the question is, do we inherit their "not so good" qualities along with their good ones? Even though we swear never to become our parents when we set out on our parenting journeys, somewhere down the line, we hear our parents' words coming from our mouths, and we cringe. It becomes a palm to the forehead moment when we realise that the apple perhaps didn't fall far from the tree after all. The beauty of doing this work is that we can choose which parts of our parents we want to keep for ourselves and those from which we want to learn. Even though we may hear our parents' voices coming involuntarily from our mouths, it can actually make us smile when we gain a deeper respect and love for them, understanding from where they have come.

My dad was an extremely handsome man, especially in his youth, but unfortunately, I look nothing like him. In fact, you couldn't even tell I was half Chinese to look at. I may not have inherited my dad's looks, but I feel very Chinese on the inside. The funny thing is that both of my sisters look more Chinese and feel more Italian while I look more Italian and feel more Chinese. They are very much Italian mammas, at their happiest with aprons on and wooden spoons in hand. They don't feel the same deep connection with our oriental origins. I love everything Chinese, including the food, traditions, and philosophy, which I undoubtedly inherited from my dad.

My dad and I had a special bond because both he and I had determination, drive, and an innate passion for our work, and I believe I got that from him. To be honest, he had a special bond with each of us, but he and I understood each other's passion, which enabled us to connect deeply. He was so proud of me for starting my own business at only 21-years of age and for following in his footsteps, probably because he saw himself in me. Other than his passion, I inherited his openness when it comes to demonstrating my love and affection for others; it just feels so natural for me to tell people how much they mean to me.

Whatever we think we inherited from our parents – our looks, quirks, personality traits, or values – whether good or bad, we have to accept and take responsibility for them. We may have inherited parts of our parents, but we are not *them*. Once we understand that we have control over who we are through our actions, behaviours, thoughts, and feelings, we are able to decide for ourselves whether to let these good and bad qualities become ruling factors in our lives.

How did your father influence your life for the better?

By now, you've probably gathered how important my dad was to me, so I won't bore you with more stories about what a wonderful influence he was in my life. Instead, I'll talk about how we influence our children's lives using my personal story as an example. Until we consciously look at our own lives and behaviours, we cannot see the impact we have on the lives of our children. Many of us go through periods in life unconsciously, reacting to life instead of living it purposefully, completely unaware of the possible repercussions of our behaviours. It may feel natural and acceptable to us, but until we are able to see the truth of who we are, we go through life blindly.

This understanding came to me in a revelation at one of my lowest points, when life had become too much for me. The light literally went out inside of me, and I was in a very dark place. I was a good, kind, and thoughtful person, setting a good example to my children – or so I thought. I'd been so busy tending to my family's every need that I lost myself somewhere along the way. Even though I continued to force a smile on my face whenever I was out and about, most days, I was in a flood of helpless tears, feeling completely lost and alone. I told myself that the best of my life had already passed, and I secretly wished my life would end soon; I was lost in the torment of my soul.

Then, one day, I was sitting at my kitchen table, eating dinner with my kids, and it was like I could see outside of myself, looking in as my tears dripped onto my plate. I came to the sharp realisation that by accepting this as my life, I was showing my kids this was an acceptable way to live, and I started to imagine how I'd feel if this were in one of my kids' futures, and it was the slap-in-the-face wakeup call I needed. It was *not* acceptable. Was that how I wanted to influence my kids' lives? Was I being the person I wanted them to grow up to be? I made a pact with myself on the spot to get my life back, that it was not too late. I was ready for a rebirth, and it all began with the decision to change.

I often wish I could sit with my parents to find out about similar lightbulb moments in their lives. This is why I write for my kids, and why I am guiding you through writing yours. We may know our family's history, as in who our ancestors were, where we came from, names and dates, but do we know what was really going on inside their minds and hearts or the state of their emotional wellbeing? Do we know why they behaved the way they did? Did they live their lives unconsciously or consciously? We may never know; however, our children will get a peek into our hearts and souls through our words. Simply being here to write your legacy speaks volumes, and it will influence your family for the better.

WHAT EXPECTATIONS DID YOU HAVE
OF YOUR PARENTS?

As each of us transitioned into parenthood – ourselves and our parents alike – we had a picture in our minds of what our families would look like and the kind of parents we were wanted to be, but nothing could prepare us for the reality of parenting. We could read every parenting book ever written or work extensively with children and families, but until we experienced parenthood for ourselves, we had no idea of the physical and emotional challenges that it brought. We anticipated the joy, love, and even hard work, but when reality sets in, it can be quite different.

When we have a fixed idea in our minds of how family life is meant to be, and our lives do not turn out as we expected, it can cause us distress. For example, if our idea of a happy family consists of a mother, father, and three kids, and that doesn't happen to us for some reason, we can feel cheated, and pain can enter our lives. It is good to have vision and direction in life, but it is the unfulfilled expectations that cause us pain. As children, if we feel our parents should be a certain way, and they do not live up to our expectations, we also tend to suffer to some level.

If we had an image in our minds that a mother should cook, clean, and be cheerful, fun, and full of life, but she was so busy trying to make ends meet that she couldn't possibly be all we expected of her, would we think less of her?

Most of us grow up unaware of underlying family difficulties; therefore, we make up our own reasons as to why our mothers were not picture-perfect in our eyes. The same goes for our fathers. We may have had an image of a strong, powerful head of the family, going out to work to provide for his family and come home cheerful at the end of the day with outstretched arms, ready to dedicate the rest of the evening to his family, but this is not real life. The truth is that we all face life, health, relationship, financial, and emotional challenges at times. Perhaps our parents had jobs they hated because they had bills to pay and mouths to feed. Perhaps they were so worn out after many years of broken sleep, putting aside their needs and desires to care for us, their demanding children, resulting in their expectations for family life being less than perfect. Sadly, some people carry resentment towards their parents for their entire lives because their expectations were not met as children. This is why I love that we are going through our lives here, to clarify the reality of life and release our grip on the past.

In my dad's memoirs, he tells a story of when I was 13 and wanted to go on a school trip to Italy. I seemingly begged and cried to go on the trip, and he was broken-hearted because he was on the verge of bankruptcy and felt like such a failure because he couldn't afford to send me. As I read his memoirs some ten years later, tears rolled down my face because I went on that school trip to Italy, unaware of the pain he'd experienced. He had to borrow money from family members so he could send me, which broke my heart as I know how hard it was for him to ask for help. Thankfully, my dad was still alive when I read his words, and I went running to him, crying, his notebook in hand, saying, "Dad, why didn't you tell me about this? I would have understood if you had sat me down and explained that we had no money." He replied, "Darling, it wasn't your problem; it was mine."

Even though my dad lived up to my expectations of him and never let me down, I now wonder whether he made a wise choice; however, he had to live up to his own expectations for himself as a father, to bring himself peace of heart and mind.

As you contemplate the expectations you had of your parents, consider their upbringing and what they felt they lacked in their childhoods that made them the kind of parents they were. Just as we all demonstrate our love in different ways, we also have expectations of what a good parent is. My mum's idea of being a good parent was raising strong, healthy, kind, and resilient children. My dad's was providing for us and making us happy. They both succeeded.

How did your parents treat each other, and what impact did that have on you?

Romance and relationships are not as they're portrayed in the movies. Well, perhaps they are for a time, but you don't often get to see the part when the love-struck couple settles into a normal life complete with work, kids, bills to pay, meals to cook, and a house to clean. We all dream of having enough money to live the life of our dreams without having to deal with the monotony of daily routines. This is, however, real life, and everyone has to face periods of monotony that life sometimes brings. We have all struggled with life not being as we envisioned it at times, and our parents would have, too.

Parenting is the hardest yet most important work most of us will ever do in our lives. Bringing children into the world is a massive responsibility, as is raising them to be physically and emotionally balanced. At times, this responsibility, alongside all the others, can take a toll on personal relationships. As we become overwhelmed with life's pressures, we often take out our stress on those who are closest to us. This doesn't make our behaviour acceptable, but it does, perhaps, make it understandable.

My parents used to work together, running a restaurant, so you can imagine the pressure they would have experienced. At times, they screamed at each other in the middle of the weekend dinner rush with the restaurant at full capacity; however, at the end of the day, they often sat down with a glass of wine or a gin and tonic and chatted. My parents always talked, which is probably why their marriage lasted.

My dad often bought my mum flowers, and on their wedding anniversary, he'd buy her one red rose for each year they were married. My mum loved it, even though she was not the romantic type. As she did not openly show her affection for him, I grew up thinking that he loved her more than she loved him. One weekend when I was in my early 20s, I took my mum for a weekend away, and we had a heart-to-heart about love and relationships. I remember saying to her, "You don't really love Dad, do you? You're only with him because you have to be, aren't you?"

She burst out laughing and said, "Nadia, of course I love your father. I love him very much, but our relationship is private and personal, between him and me."

I was completely shocked as I had no idea how much she really loved him. I had used my personal relationship with my mum to cloud my judgement of her relationship with my dad, and I had it all wrong. I loved seeing this loving, gentle side of my mum while talking about my dad, and to be honest, it made me see their relationship in a new light, and I think my mum did, too. Soon after, I noticed my mum being more openly loving towards my dad. I am unsure whether it was due to our conversation or because I'd become more aware of the love between them.

As you think about how your parents treated each other, consider the external pressures they were under and their ability to handle their emotions at specific times in their relationship. There is no denying that relationships take work, time, patience, and forgiveness, but when there is love, respect, and a willingness to grow together, we can get through. Whether your parents were openly loving and affectionate towards each other, at each other's throats or didn't make it through as a couple, think about the impact their relationship had on your relationships.

What did your mother tell you about her childhood that left an impression on you?

Mum and Dad were children during World War Two, and they both had stories to tell of life with little or no food. Because of this, they understood how blessed they were to have their daily bread, so-to-speak, and they instilled an attitude of gratitude in our lives. Listening to my mother talk and seeing her tears made me realise how much she had suffered as a child. She told me that, as a toddler, she also refused to eat and was so weak that she didn't walk until she was five-years-old, which is probably why she worried about me so much. The doctors had told her parents that she would probably never walk due to not having enough nourishment for her bones to grow and develop properly, but she proved them all wrong. My mum may have had a tough childhood due to health issues, growing up during the war, having to survive on very little, and bringing up her brothers and sisters, but she was a fighter – all four-foot 11 inches of her. Her parents were very strict with her – if she said or did anything wrong, she was punished by having to go to bed without dinner. Other times, if she didn't like the meal she was offered, she would not get any more food until she had eaten what was put in front of her. So, if she didn't eat her dinner, she would get the same plate for breakfast. After relating this experience to us, I realised why she was so determined that my sisters and I were always well-fed and why she and I used to battle over food. She had carried her beliefs and conditioning around food into her parenting, and subconsciously passed learned behaviour on to me, perpetuating a pattern of beliefs.

By recalling her stories and understanding this aspect of my mother's upbringing, I was able to appreciate her attitude towards me and my relationship with food. As a child, what I had believed to be anger at me for not eating was actually my mother's fear for my health and wellbeing, which was motivated by her love for me, and not a lack thereof.

As you think about what your mother told you about her own childhood, take the time to consider how this may have shaped her parenting skills and her relationship with you.

What did your father tell you about his childhood that left an impression on you?

Not everyone was fortunate enough to have both parents in their lives, but I can imagine that most people have some knowledge of their parents. This knowledge may only be in the form of stories from the past or bitter memories, but it is some knowledge, nevertheless.

We can carry these stories and memories with us subconsciously throughout our lives, and we tend to use them to shape our journeys through life. Our choices are made using the knowledge we acquire, so if our conditioning did not serve us or the knowledge we have is not correct, we are bound to make some wrong choices along the way. For example, if one of our parents grew up fatherless because his/her father had left, his/her fear of abandonment may have been passed onto us, so what we grew up believing wasn't necessarily the truth of life, but that which was passed on due to conditioning from our parents.

The story my father wrote in his memoirs about his father is the story that pierces my soul the deepest. He talks about Japanese soldiers beating my grandad and leaving him for dead simply because he was secretly fishing in the river, desperate to feed his starving family. My grandad didn't die instantly, but he never recovered from his injuries, and at the age of 44, he died in the arms of my 17-year-old dad, passing on to him the responsibility of taking care of the family as the oldest son. When I read his words, my heart broke for him, and something within me knew I would be with my dad when it was his time to go, and I got my wish.

For three months, my dad laid in a hospital bed as his body slowly shut down. It was the 8th of January, 2011, and his time was almost up. He was no longer able to speak or move, but I could sense his pain and the torment in his soul. He was so brave for holding on, but I knew he was ready to leave this earth. He was not scared to die, but I knew his love for us was holding him back. He was reluctant to leave us, his three little girls, without their dad to take care of them. So, I crawled into his hospital bed, laid beside him, held him in my arms, and whispered in his ear, "I'm here for you, Dad, and there's nothing to be afraid of. You've been an amazing dad, and it's okay to leave now and go to Mum. God will always watch over us, and we'll all be fine. We'll always love you." The moment I gave him permission to leave, he died peacefully in my arms.

My wonderful Dad had spent more than half of his life being a father, and letting go couldn't have been easy. He knew what it was like to go through life without a father, and he didn't want us to have to go through what he did, but with my permission and me holding him tightly, we let each other silently go.

Think about the stories of your childhood that have been passed down to you and how they have shaped your thoughts and beliefs about life. Have they inspired you to become the person you believe you can be, or have they blocked happiness from flowing to you? Are you reluctant to let go of an old, limiting belief due to fear, or are you ready to exercise your faith and trust?

WHAT DID YOU DO FOR FUN AS A FAMILY WHEN GROWING UP?

We are often so focused on what needs to be fixed in our lives that we forget about what was and still is magical about them. As children, we are more fun-focused. As we grow and start taking on responsibilities, fun can often take a back seat, but it is an essential part of life, so we need to make time for family fun, no matter our age. Just as our ideas about love and parental responsibilities are subjective, so is our idea of fun, which also stems from our childhood.

Growing up, our family fun usually centred around food. Given that my dad was an amazing chef, and my mum was a typical Italian mamma, it seemed inevitable. Even though food wasn't much fun for me unless it was party food, sweets, or ice cream, it certainly was for my sisters. One of them remembers clearly what we ate as children and where we ate but not much else. We still laugh about it now, how two sisters can live pretty much the same lives yet have a whole different perspective. Both of my sisters have only happy memories of our childhood, but because I was unhappy on the inside, my memories of childhood are different. Let me be clear: I did not have an unhappy childhood, but because I was so deep and highly sensitive and didn't feel as if I fit in, my perception was one of unhappiness. However, when I consciously focused on the fun I had with my family as a child, the memories came flooding in.

As my parents were far from their families' homes, they built a wonderful network of friends in Norwich, England, which made our younger years so much fun. We were always surrounded by friends who felt like family. My parents were kind and generous people, so we often had a houseful of people being fed delicious food. We did not need a reason to celebrate to have a lot of food and people around; it was simply my parents celebrating life and sharing their love and joy with their friends.

Even though my mum was an extrovert and loved socialising, she hated having her photo taken, so there were not many recordings of fun times to trigger happy memories. Because I have hardly any childhood photos of us together, I wanted that to be different for my children, which forced me to overcome my own insecurities around having my photo taken. My desire to keep my children's happy memories alive was bigger than my insecurities, which made me put my fears aside, face the camera lens, and smile to capture our family's fun moments. My children may not appreciate their "snap happy" mother now, but I know, hand-on-heart, that one day they will look back at the hundreds, if not thousands of photos I have taken over the years, smile, and say, "We had a fun childhood."

HOW DID YOU FEEL ABOUT YOUR SIBLINGS? IF YOU WERE AN ONLY CHILD, HOW DID YOU FEEL ABOUT NOT HAVING SIBLINGS?

All relationships need to be nurtured and take some work to maintain, but my relationship with my sisters is easy, and I know they accept me for who I am and love me unconditionally. They have known me my entire life, so there is no hiding my true self from them. When I am sad or broken, I run to them. When all is going well, I share my wins with them…first. They are my soulmates, and no matter what happens, I know I can trust them with all my heart, but that was not the case when I was younger.

There they were, these two beautiful, long-haired, raven beauties, and then there was me, with my "short back and sides". I felt different from them, and so, I felt left out. Marisa, my big sister, was the beautiful, clever, obedient child, Gisella was the beautiful, sweet, and funny one who got away with everything through humour, and then there was me, the piggy in the middle, so to speak, never able to catch the ball, desperately trying to be noticed, but never feeling quite good enough. Bedtimes, when we were small, were not about bedtime stories and hugs – they were about me getting shouted at and smacked for laughing when Gisella made us all laugh after we were in bed. On top of that, being a highly sensitive child, I took everything to heart. I was a deep little soul, even then, always curious about the meaning of life, but I never ever shared my thoughts. Like many middle children, I felt as if I were the black sheep of the family.

In hindsight, I can see that I was the one who set myself apart, out of fear of not being accepted or understood. I was jealous of my sisters and wanted to be like them, but I simply wasn't. Like most families, we did not talk about our feelings, but I do remember my dad turning to me out of the blue one day, saying, "Nadia, you're not adopted, you know!"

I was shocked because that was the exact thought going through my mind at the time, and I wondered whether he could read my thoughts, but he obviously sensed my distress – *he* was my dad, after all. Even though I hadn't said a word, I felt as if I had finally been heard.

As we grew up, we also grew closer as sisters and as a family as a whole. We didn't think much of it at the time, but even as teens and going into our 20s, we ate together as a family almost every day, went on trips together, spent our days off together, and our family home was a gathering place for all of our friends to eat and socialise together, just as it had been when we were young. We may not have been the perfect family, but we were very much a happy one.

When my sisters and I gathered around my dad on his deathbed, he made us promise to make an effort to be a part of each other's lives and stick together as a family. Of course, we promised, but we didn't need to because we were, and always will be, bound in love. Family, to me, is one of life's greatest blessings, but in order for us to reap those blessings, we first have to look within and rid ourselves of the burdens we carry from childhood – our fears and insecurities – and learn to forgive each other and ourselves for being less than perfect to sustain and maintain those family bonds.

This is another reason why I write – to encourage you to do your own inner-work to break through these blocks, allowing the love and joy to flow freely, releasing the wonderful memories that underpin your legacy.

Question 25

HOW AFFECTIONATE WERE YOUR PARENTS WITH YOU AND YOUR SIBLINGS?

Love and affection have so many different faces, and it can be demonstrated in multiple ways, depending on the kind of people we are as well as subject to childhood conditioning. We all see aspects of life in our unique ways, and therefore, each of us reacts differently, so love can be misinterpreted and misunderstood.

Even though my mother was not openly affectionate, as I mentioned earlier, she showed her love and affection through cooking lovely meals and taking care of us. I grew up feeling unloved by my mum because my idea of love was hugs, kisses, and her undivided attention, but that simply wasn't who my mum was. I very much doubt she would have purposefully withheld affection from me as a way of punishment or control, but her lack of physical touch affected me deeply. My sisters grew up feeling completely loved by my mum, even without hugs, so it was not her lack of demonstrating her love for us that was the problem; rather, it was my need for physical affection. If she knew how I had felt at the time, I am sure she would have behaved differently towards me, but she didn't know any better. She simply loved us the only way she knew how. Dad was, however, the opposite, and he would hug me openly as a demonstration of his love; therefore, I grew up thinking he loved me more than Mum did.

I am very much a "touchy-feely" kind of person, which comes naturally to me, but for some people, being that way is what my kids would call "cringy". My older sister laughs at me when I visit her in our hometown because I go around hugging everyone I know. She is nothing like me and more like my mother – she does not do hugs unless she really has to, but that does not mean she loves any less. She is simply less "touchy-feely" than I am, although, to be honest, everyone is less "touchy-feely" than I am.

Just as people express love differently, they also want it demonstrated to them differently. For some, love is tactile, being held, touched, and hugged. Others need words, and others need gifts. As a result of these different ways of expressing and receiving love, it can, at times, go unnoticed. Looking back, I can see how much my mum loved me. I can also see that by not eating her lovingly prepared meals, I was, in a way, rejecting her. Food was her way of showing love, and my sisters accepted and understood that, so they felt her love. Because my idea of love was physical affection, I didn't understand her demonstration of love, and I missed out on it.

As a mother, I not only shower my kids with love and affection in the form of hugs and kisses, I also try to be fully present in their lives, to make the time to understand the people they are becoming, and to take care of their emotional and physical health. Because of my health issues as a result of not eating healthily as a child, I have made my kids' health and diet a priority. My children have grown up on home-cooked meals, including whole grains, fruit, vegetables, and no sugar. In order for them to have the sweet treats that all children love, I lovingly made them homemade, naturally-sweetened desserts, biscuits, and ice cream and continue to do so. They may not recognise this as the expression of my love that it is, but their health and wellbeing is far more important to me than their adoring love for me!

What parenting mistakes do you believe your parents made, and how did their mistakes make you stronger?

I believe that everything that has ever happened to us has happened for a reason. The pain and suffering we go through are there to teach us valuable lessons. This may be hard to take in, especially if you have had a particularly challenging life, but we can either choose to learn and grow from the past or let it destroy us, it is that simple. None of us is perfect, and we never will be – not our grandparents, parents, ourselves, or our children. We can do our best to strive for purity and greatness, but we all make mistakes. We are here to experience life as human beings, so if we are all perfect, we would be robbed of experiencing the fulfilment of personal growth and evolution.

I do not know about you, but I have made many mistakes as a parent. We are not given an instruction manual for parenting, and even with all the advice from books, our parents, and our friends, we mostly learn from trial and error. I read every parenting book I could get my hands on as soon as I found out I was pregnant so I could be the best mother I could be, yet I still made mistakes.

With my first child, Leon, like most parents, I made sure he was always clean and didn't touch anything dirty. I was obsessed with him avoiding coming into contact with germs. One day, he fell over and landed flat on his face, ending up with a face-full of scratches. I asked him why he hadn't put his hands down to stop his fall, and he replied that he didn't want to get his hands dirty. *I'd done that!* I had created a fear in him so deep-seated that he would rather be injured than get dirty. It was fortunate I was able to see the error of my parenting ways, and I made a commitment to be a more conscious parent instead of a fearful one. This, of course, was only one of the many mistakes I made and continue to make with my growing teens. We have to remember that every age and stage is a learning process for both parent and child, so mistakes will be made, just as our parents made mistakes.

I spent a big part of my life focusing on the mistakes my mother made with me, blaming her for my shortcomings, clinging onto my childhood insecurities, but the truth is that she had done nothing wrong. If I could go back and have a conversation with my mother about what she could have given my younger self, I would say, "Dedicate some one-on-one time with her and really listen to her. She needs your love, affection, and undivided attention to know that you love her."

However, if my mother *had* loved me the way I wanted, my life would not have unfolded the way it has, and perhaps this book would never have been written. The exercise of researching my legacy meant that I discovered her love for me which positively influenced my experience of love and motherhood. Finding light and truth within my personal history has given me the strength and power to shed some light on yours – it was simply meant to be.

Question 27

DO YOU THINK YOUR PARENTS WERE THE BEST PARENTS THEY COULD BE, BASED ON THE KNOWLEDGE AND EXPERIENCE THEY HAD? HOW DID THEY INFLUENCE YOUR OWN PARENTING?

In this day and age with literally everything we need to know at our fingertips, are we doing our best? Are we feeding our children a good diet to give them sufficient nourishment to sustain and maintain their good health in the future? Are we the examples of goodness, light, and joy that we know we should be as parents? Are we living the lives of our dreams to encourage our growing children to follow their hearts in pursuit of their own hopes and dreams in life? No? Then why on earth did we expect our own parents to do everything right?

I believe we are all doing the best we can with the level of knowledge and experience each of us has. Of course, we make mistakes, but none of us deliberately set out to make our kids' lives difficult, but what we say and do has an impact on everyone's life we touch, and not just our children. How we behave, react, speak, and interact with the human race, in general, emits a certain energy we put out into the world.

If we do not acknowledge our pain and keep ourselves weighed down with chains of the past, we will never be truly free. Forgiveness is the key to unlocking these chains, but we first have to be willing to let go of the negative energy and free ourselves. There is a famous quote that says, "Holding onto anger is like drinking poison and expecting the other person to die," meaning that we are only hurting ourselves when we lack forgiveness. Forgiveness is not condoning undesired past behaviours; it is about loving yourself enough to let things go.

My parents were wonderful parents, and they did the very best they could and then some. I knew they loved me, but because of my insecurities, I didn't feel good enough, and I put limitations on experiencing that love. By doing this work to understand who I am, I have let go of these limitations, leaving me with a feeling of tremendous gratitude for the parents which whom I was blessed, who allowed me to be an example for my own children.

If you are still stuck in old, negative thought patterns like I was, consider what you may not have been able to see then that you can see now. Be encouraged to let go of negative thoughts you may have about their parenting skills, and imagine yourself in their shoes with their level of knowledge and understanding. Think about the benefits you gained from having the kind of parents you had, the wisdom you received, and how your experience made you a better parent.

WHAT KIND OF PARENT ARE YOU? WHAT PARENTING ADVICE WOULD YOU OFFER TO HELP OTHERS AVOID MAKING THE SAME MISTAKES AS YOU?

Mistakes are inevitable and an essential part of our personal growth, so the sooner we learn from our mistakes, the better. We can't go back to change the past, but we can acknowledge our mistakes and do what we can to undo any damage or harm we have unwittingly caused. This book is one of love and inner-peace between parents and children of all ages. It is a tool for healing our inner wounds, enabling us to become even better parents by being examples of change.

Now that I am free from my negative thought patterns (even though they pop their heads in from time to time), I can see the mistakes I made in my parenting. I was such a hands-on mother, and I dedicated every waking hour to my kids' happiness and wellbeing. Why was that wrong? Because I was so focused on being the best mother I could be that I had failed to take care of "me". What kind of example was I setting my children, that I was not important as a mother, and that their lives were worth more than mine? At the time, I truly believed that but I hadn't taken that one day, they would be parents, too, into account, and I was showing them that it was okay to neglect yourself for others, essentially telling them that caring for children means that *you* do not matter.

Our job as parents is not to make our children happy, but rather, to teach them not only how to survive in life, but to thrive, teaching them how to deal with life's challenges and become strong, happy, and resilient adults. The best way to do this – in fact, the best way to teach anything – is by example. Accepting a life of misery or not pursuing our dreams and aspirations would be teaching them that it is okay to give up and settle for a life that does not bring them joy – is that what we want for our children?

My advice to you is to become the person you desire your children to be. Instead of hoping, wishing, and pushing them to make the most of their lives and health, *be* the example that shows them what a happy, kind, compassionate, and healthy human being looks like.

Loving our children takes more than just taking care of their physical and emotional needs – it is also teaching them to love the innermost parts of who they are and to value themselves as human beings, and the best way to do that is by leading the way.

Do you believe your parents felt happy and loved as children, and how do you think that affected their lives and their futures?

The world has changed dramatically over the past 100 years or so, and as a result, you would think we would be a happier generation with all of the home comforts with which we live with today; however, I do not believe this to be true. We may have had more than our parents growing up, but did that make us any happier? Because our children have more than we ever had, are they happier still? Even though both of my parents had troublesome childhoods, growing up during the war with so much fear and scarcity, I believe they were happy children. Without a doubt, they would have had their own, personal challenges and struggled with their sense of self, but don't we all?

A lot of what we learned at school taught us nothing about real life, but merely filled our minds with facts and figures, but imagine how different our lives would have been if we had been taught how to manage our minds by developing our emotional intelligence. Not only would we have the skills to better deal with our thoughts, feelings, and emotions, we would have learned that outside factors and other people are not responsible for our happiness; we are. This goes for us, our parents, and all the generations that have gone before us. My parents had very little and lost many family members during the war, but it ultimately made them appreciate the gift of life more to become happy adults.

My mum rarely opened up to me about her insecurities, but from hearing her constantly call herself ugly, I knew she had some deep-rooted conditioning within her, which I ultimately inherited. I also know she felt unloved by the way she got upset when her family in Italy didn't contact her. She would say things such as, "It's always me that calls them. Nobody ever thinks of me." It makes me wonder whether my mum "ran away" from her family because she felt she wasn't loved or appreciated, but sadly, I will never know what was truly in her heart and mind. As she got older and we became closer, we both opened up to each other. I told her how I felt as a child, and she quietly listened and cried without trying to defend herself, and I began to know and understand the beautiful soul she was. We began to heal the old wounds between us, but we did not know that her time was almost up. I still had so much to learn about who she really was, but sadly, it was not meant to be.

Over a decade after she died, Gisella and I went to visit one of my mum's sisters that she didn't necessarily get on with very well. She had not seen us since we were children, and the first thing she said was, "You're both so beautiful, which is surprising, considering you came from your mum." We said nothing as we were brought up to be well-mannered, but I felt my mum's pain and understood more about what had shaped her conditioning. I may not have had the time with my mum I had hoped for to know her completely, but I feel the essence of her love and sensitive heart beating inside my chest; she lives on in me.

How did you feel as a first-time parent, and what were your biggest challenges?

As my mum had died suddenly when my first child was only a year old, I didn't only lose her love; I also lost my lifeline for guidance. I had turned to her for everything in that first year and was on the phone with her multiple times a day, to get advice or to have someone to listen to my challenges as a new mother, and when she was no longer around, my whole world fell apart. She was a strong-willed, strong-bodied woman with no underlying health issues. She was alive and well one day and gone the next, and I was left feeling shocked, lost, and very confused. I had naively thought I still had so much time to ask her about life and parenting, but that was not our fate.

For me, being a first-time parent was a mixture of pure joy mixed with fear. The joy for obvious reasons, but the fear that I now had something so precious in my life that I could lose was equally as strong. I'd stay awake for hours watching him, making sure he was still breathing, and I wouldn't let him out of my sight.

When Leon was only six-weeks-old, I went for a quick shower, leaving him with his dad, but when I came out, they were both gone. I went into panic mode, and my overthinking mind went into overdrive, thinking up all the horrible and unbearable things that might have happened. Twenty long minutes passed before my husband came strolling back with the pram. He had decided to take our baby for a walk, probably to give me a break, yet I went ballistic! The feelings I had were out of control, and I was acting irrationally, having a full-blown, adult tantrum. If he had only told me he was going out, I would have been okay…maybe.

I can look back on the scene and laugh now at how unreasonable I was, but at that moment in time, I was overcome with fear. With the hormones and lack of sleep, I could not have been the easiest person to deal with, but nothing could come between my baby and me, not even his dad.

Losing my mum left a huge hole in my heart, especially as a new mum, but I learned a valuable lesson from her sudden death: that tomorrow is not guaranteed. I understand the reality of our mortality, and this is now a guiding force in my life. What we write concerning our experiences as first-time parents may be the lifelines our children and grandchildren need in the future, so we have to make our words count by being open and honest with ourselves and them through baring our souls. It may not always be easy, but it is for a worthy cause: our children.

Question 31

KNOWING WHAT YOU KNOW NOW ABOUT THE CHALLENGES AND RESPONSIBILITIES OF PARENTING, IF YOU COULD DO IT ALL AGAIN, WHAT WOULD YOU DO DIFFERENTLY?

We have only one life, only one chance at making our lives count, and the same goes for parenting. The trouble is that we go into parenting blind, and we learn as we go, so we make mistakes. One of my closest friends has seven children. She is a wonderful mother, but that is probably because she has had a lot of practice and has worked out what works and what does not. The reality is that most of us do not get as much practice. That being said, every child is an individual, unique soul, so mistakes are an inevitable part of parenting. As soon as we think we have mastered one part of parenting or one particular age or stage, our children grow, and a whole other set of challenges appears. As well as being parents, we have to be nurses, cooks, psychologists, teachers, and entertainers, to name a few, so it is no wonder we all make mistakes. Parenting is not the easiest job. Nevertheless, few would give up the privilege of being a parent, even though it may have crossed our minds, mid-tantrum in the middle of a supermarket or during a teenage meltdown.

Personally, if I were to start again, I would worry less and try to be a more relaxed parent. Like a lot of other parents, I worried about everything, and the more I worried, the more stressed we all became. I would focus on what could go wrong in every situation, in essence, creating fear and negative energy. As an example, when my son was learning to ride a bike without his training wheels on the driveway of our house, I would shout out, "Watch out for the lamppost. Don't hit the lamppost!" All I was doing was bringing attention to the lamppost and what could go wrong, and every time I mentioned it, he would steer towards it!

I learned from my mistakes but not before instilling my own anxieties into my children's minds. I had "inherited" a mind-set of worry from my parents and was inadvertently passing it on to my children, but when I knew better, I did better.

We think that it is "normal" to worry about our children, but worry is simply a collection of stories we have made up of what *could* go wrong. They are negative thoughts and fears *we* have brought to life, but only in our minds. Once we quieten our minds and tell ourselves there is no evidence to support the prediction in our minds, we are able to bring a more peaceful energy to our lives and that of our children.

As you think and write about the things you would change and begin to acknowledge the mistakes you have made, remember there is no such thing as a perfect parent. This work is not about accepting blame or shame for mistakes made – it is about acknowledging our humanness, seeing our lives and ourselves in a better light, inspiring us to make the necessary adjustments to know better and do better. Again, leading by example.

How did becoming a parent change you as a person?

Becoming a parent comes with such an array of emotions and/or a shift in emotions, ranging from infinite love to overwhelming fear as we witness the miracles of our new-born children. Along with the intense love and joy comes a reality check of responsibility when taking care of the beautiful, brand-new human beings we have made. The bundles of joy we hold in our arms change us. How could they not?

When I was young, I didn't want to get married or have children. My reasoning was that because I was unhappy, I would not put another being through the same torment as me. However, that all changed the day my nephew was born. The minute I set eyes on that beautiful baby boy only a few hours after he was born, my heart melted, and I fell instantly in love for the first time in my life. As if a switch had clicked on, I knew then and there that I wanted to be a mother.

For me, becoming a mother was a calling from my soul, and I loved every minute of it. It was hard work, and I had the usual struggles, but I made it my literal full-time job. It gave my life a sense of meaning and purpose, and I knew the work I was doing was truly valuable. There is no greater responsibility in life than being a parent, and it was my duty and privilege to bring two beautiful pure souls into the world. It was my job to guide them, love them, support them, teach them, and keep them safe physically, emotionally, and spiritually.

The challenging part was when they started to grow up and become more independent, and I was forced to grow as they did. I had to learn to let them go and to be free to make their own choices, good and bad.

I like to think that being a parent made me a better human being. My children are my greatest teachers as they stretch and challenge me to become the best version of me, even though I don't always succeed. What I have learned most is that personal growth is and always will be a work in progress for us all, that change is inevitable, and it must be embraced.

Describe what you were like as a teenager and your view of the world back then. What advice would you give your teenage self?

Were you shy or outgoing? Were you popular, or did you feel insignificant? Were you ambitious and ready to grab life with both hands or fearful of real life out in the world? Many of us had no idea of who we were or what we wanted from life and went through a bit of an identity crisis. We felt pressure to grow up when we didn't feel ready. As young children, we were relatively carefree, being taken care of, fed, clothed, and nurtured, but within a short space of time, we were forced to make important life and work decisions for the future.

As I am now raising teenagers, my own memories of being a teen have come flooding back. I feel so much sadness and regret for the way I treated my mum at times, but as I look at my kids and feel the pain of their behaviour towards me, I smile to myself and think: "karma!" Nevertheless, I stand strong in the fact I have built strong foundations for them, just as my parents did for my sisters and me. Whatever storms life brings, they and I will survive it. My work to help my children to become resilient and strong-willed adults and for them to stand up for that in which they believe sometimes comes back to bite me on the bum. As they question my guidance, however, I am reminded that the apple did not fall far from the tree – I turned out okay, and they will, too.

My teens were certainly a time of personal discovery and learning, even with all the mistakes and poor decisions I made.

I do, sometimes, wish I had more guidance, and because of that, I decided to write the book, *My Growing Heart*. It is a guide not just for my children, but for all children, to help them on the journey towards understanding who they are and what they want to be. I essentially wrote the book I needed to read as a teenager, one that would have enabled me to be more confident, to own my emotions, and teach me how to love and value myself as a human being.

Now that you have lived and learnt some life lessons for yourself, contemplate the advice you would have liked to have been given as a teen that would have made life a little easier for you.

What was your fashion sense like as a teenager, and what influenced you to dress the way you did?

I'll bet this question made you smile. Writing this legacy is meant to do just that, and it will do the same for your family when they read it. When you think back to what you thought was fashionable, I am sure you now find it laughable.

As teens seeking our own identities, we naively thought our worth needed validation from others, especially through how we looked and what we wore. One minute we would feel like the bee's knees in our fashionable outfit, hoping to make everyone jealous, the next, we would feel like an outsider, insignificant and unworthy if we weren't on-trend. The world hasn't changed much in that sense, but in the current age of social media, teens are under so much more pressure.

I am grateful we did not have access to cell phone cameras to record some of the horrendous fashion choices I made. When I see some of the outfits teens wear these days, I laugh to myself and imagine them looking back from the future, saying, "Did I really wear that? I look ridiculous!" I know this because I was very much a fashion victim. In fact, the only reason I worked washing dishes, was so I could afford to buy myself these ridiculous outfits to feel significant. I should have saved my money.

The thing is, as a teen, 80's fashion wasn't my style. I remember dreaming about being 40, so I could wear beautiful, stylish dresses and high heels. I loved actress Sophia Loren's look: classic, chic, feminine, and very stylish. My mum was a dressmaker and also loved stylish clothes, which is probably where I got my inspiration. From time to time, she would spontaneously buy me some lovely clothes. Once, when I was about 12, she bought me a lovely cord pencil skirt with a little split up the front, and I loved it. When I wore it, though, two of my friends told me I looked like a tart. I went running home crying to my mum, and she called my friends in to give them a good telling off, making them apologise to me! I remember feeling so loved that day.

I was so happy that my mum was brave enough to stand up for me, and from then on, I wore that skirt with pride.

I used to go into my mum's wardrobe, put on her dresses and heels, and parade around the house, but as a teen, I knew I would have been laughed at if I went out dressed like a lady. Despite this and my love for elegance and style, sadly I settled for whatever were the season's looks, whether that meant wearing odd fluorescent socks or the laced and leathered look to be like Madonna. For this reason, in the book, *My Growing Heart*, I talk about how, as teens, it is important to be proud of who you are and not get sucked into a world of comparing and wanting to be like others.

How did it feel to fall in love for the first time?

Young love cannot be beaten, that innocence and wonder in life that brings smiles to our faces and puts a bounce in our steps; the anticipation of our first kisses, holding hands while running through fields of green, and smiling and laughing in the sunshine. We wish. Most of us likely experienced a quick kiss at the back of the bike shed where no one could see, wondering if it was love.

Despite love and loving relationships being such an important part of life, we rarely speak openly about them. It is a touchy subject, and neither parent nor child really wants to go there. Parents find it hard to know when to have the conversation so as not to appear to encourage entering into relationships too soon. For teens, the last people to discuss emotions with are parents. They only turn to them as a last resort, and even then, they do not really want their advice. That leaves turning to friends who are just as clueless, so it is no wonder hearts are broken repeatedly, and bad choices are made! It is also not easy to discuss matters of the heart with friends because of the fear of being the odd one out or appearing clueless. That whole period of discovering love can be a lonely time.

Speaking of my personal experiences as a teen, I came from a place of insecurity with a need to fit in, be accepted, and loved, and my friends had similar experiences. At times, we found ourselves being talked into following the crowd, which led us into situations in which we didn't want to be. I often wonder how we managed to get out relatively unharmed. Because I had gotten myself into these difficult situations, I knew I had to find my way back out, and I did so with lessons learned.

My first love was Christopher Clark, a dark-haired boy who was so handsome that all the girls loved him, including my big sister. We were six-years-old. One day, when he and I were skipping around the playground holding hands, we decided to show our teacher something amazing we'd discovered we could do. We ran up to her excitedly to share our little trick. I can still remember the look of shock and disgust on her face as she watched us turn to face each other and wiggle our tongues together. In our innocence, we had no idea that we were doing something wrong. It wasn't kissing to us – it was simply a trick that we wanted to share with her. Needless to say, after the inevitable telling off, we didn't do it again. So, there started my tumultuous journey into love. I started young and have pretty much had boyfriends my whole life. My little heart was broken time and time again, until, of course, the next boy appeared, and my heart would miraculously heal yet again.

WHAT WERE YOUR PASSIONS, GIFTS, AND TALENTS AS A YOUNG PERSON?

As children, we are full of joy and enthusiasm for life. We look at life with wonder and awe and believe anything is possible. We had the ability to dream big, and may have even wanted to be unicorns because there was no reason why we couldn't be. So, what happened to those dreams? Life happened. As we grew up and faced rejections, disappointments, and made a few wrong turns, we began to doubt our abilities and worth and started to play small, hiding our lights in fear of failure.

We stopped trusting in ourselves and started comparing ourselves to others, doubting our self-worth, worried about not being good enough. We began listening to the advice of well-meaning others who told us to make practical choices that would pay the bills instead of pursuing our passions. Day by day, week by week, month by month, year by year, our hopes and dreams for our lives became crushed until we couldn't even remember what they were anymore.

Then, one day we woke up, looked at our lives and asked ourselves "How did I get here? This wasn't the life I wanted." However, it is never too late to begin dreaming again, no matter how old we are. While there is still blood pumping through our veins, there is still time. We can't go back to relive our lives over again, but we can look within ourselves, find what ignites our souls, and start living our dreams, using our gifts and talents to bring light and joy into our lives and into the lives of others.

When I was a little girl, all I wanted to be was a hairdresser. I loved playing with and cutting my dolls' hair. I would go to the hairdresser's with anyone who would take me, and I would literally sit for hours with wide eyes, taking in all the sights, smells, and sounds. Thankfully, my parents did not try to influence my life choices, and as soon as I left school, I went to college to study hair and beauty, which I loved. It was a joy making people feel better about themselves and putting smiles on their faces. By the time I was 21, I had opened a salon with my best friend, but as I approached 30, I knew I wanted more from life. I wanted to live overseas and be a full-time mum, and that is exactly what I did, and I could not have been happier.

Through all this, I always knew I would write a book one day, but I had no idea what I would write about. As I grew and evolved with the passing years, my calling became stronger and stronger until I could no longer ignore the whisperings of my soul. I had no idea what to do or where to start, but I had a loving message bursting to come out, so I began to write. Through one step and one word at a time, my first book was born. I am telling you this to inspire and encourage you to listen to the whisperings of your soul, regardless of your age.

Success is not measured by what we have done, achieved, or accumulated in life – it is measured by how we feel. If we are at peace with who we are, spending time doing what we love, to me, that is true success.

All of your experiences, good and bad, have led you here, to this very moment, ready to awaken the joy and passion in your heart. As you recall what your gifts and talents were, think about what used to spark your enthusiasm, that about which you were passionate, what you were good at that gave you a sense of pride and put a smile on your face.

What were your dreams and aspirations for the future when you were young? How did you envision yourself as an adult living your dream life?

As we spoke about in question 36, when we are children, we have so much enthusiasm for life, but as adults, we allow our dreams to slip through our fingers. We weren't happy and enthusiastic kids because we were successful – we were happy because we had dreams and aspirations. No matter who we are, how skilled we are, or what talents we have, we can all dream and live life with passion. We may not make our fortunes at it, but we can bring joy and enthusiasm to our lives by doing what we love.

I have always been a dream chaser; it is simply who I am. Perhaps I became this way because I never felt significant as a child, but I am not one for sitting back, waiting for life to get better – I work on making it better. I was dumbfounded when I found myself in the depths of depression because I did not know who I was anymore or where I was going. When we have no dreams or direction in life, we can get stuck in the monotony of daily existence. I lost all hope, and I lost my ability to dream. Not only do dreams and aspirations give us a direction in which to move forward, but they also fuel our passions. Whether we reach our final destinations or not is irrelevant. What is important is that we live life with joy and enthusiasm. For example, through writing this book, I aspire to transform lives, to help you see the wonder and beauty within yourself, to realise your worth through writing your legacy, but the love and energy I put into my work is what is important, not the completion of the book. If I did not achieve my dream, would that make me a failure? Absolutely not, because I live each day passionately in pursuit of fulfilling my heartfelt intentions. In my eyes, I am succeeding in life! Just as happiness is not a final destination, neither is success – it is about the journey.

My life is not how I envisioned it as a child – it's better. I never dreamed of becoming a mother, living in Italy, or becoming a life coach. All I knew then was that I wanted to be a hairdresser and to be happy. Writing a book was not a childhood dream, either – it began as a tiny seed within my soul that grew and blossomed as I did.

When we live in pursuit of our current dreams – whether our dreams are to travel the world, to have happy marriages, or to write legacies for our children – we live life with purpose, growing and progressing, one step, one word, one page at a time. As you think back on your dreams and aspirations, or how you envisioned your life to be, ask yourself if those dreams are still alive within you. Have they grown and evolved to become your reality, or did you keep them hidden in fear of failure, not being good enough, or looking foolish? One of my life's mottos is "I'd rather live a life of failure than a life of regret," because, for me, the only true failure in life is never trying. As you recall what used to light you up and fuel your energy, decide whether you want to stop dreaming or if you are ready to reignite that inner light!

AS A YOUNG PERSON,

WHAT WAS YOUR DREAM JOB?

"Do what you love, and you never have to work a day in your life."
~ Marc Anthony

I love this quote. For me, it's absolutely true. I have come to realise that this is how I have lived my life. It is actually how we should all live our lives. Imagine a world where everyone does what they love, going to work with joy and enthusiasm. The effects would have an incredible impact on our ways of life, and we would all be so much happier. There would still be challenges, but to live a life in which you spend your days doing what you love would come with endless joy…and benefits. You would have more energy, patience, and love to share, and if everyone else were doing the same, the world would most definitely be a better place in which to live. The trouble is that humans strive for a life that looks good on the outside and not one that feels good on the inside. We are all unique and have our own gifts, talents, and longings of the soul, but we do not always listen to these longings and end up settling for less or striving for careers that give us financial gain and material comforts regardless of whether they bring us joy or not. We may even get attached to an end goal of becoming rich and famous, thinking we will be happy when we reach our destination, but if we don't love what we do every day, we miss out on the joy of the journey.

Because we had to make our career choices when we were teens, before our brains were fully developed, we did not necessarily have the wisdom or emotional maturity to make the right choices for our futures. We took advice from well-meaning others or chased titles or accolades in pursuit of success, but we were not taught how to stop and listen to the longing of our soul. We were not taught to seek out our passions and live in pursuit of making a difference in the world in our own unique ways through sharing our passions. Perhaps we spent years studying to give us the qualifications we needed to become financially successful, but without love and passion at the core, the job is simply a job, a means to make money.

As you think about what your dream job was, ask yourself *why* you wanted to do that for a living. What did you think it would bring to your life? Did you want to help others, make them smile, or improve their lives in some way? Did you desire to save the planet, nature, or advance the world of technology somehow? When we stop to look inside and begin to reignite that spark within, our true selves start to emerge. We may not be able to go back and start over, but we *can* draw a line in the sand and make a fresh start. It is never too late to live your dream life or pursue your dream job.

WHAT WAS YOUR FAVOURITE PASTIME GROWING UP? WHAT DID YOU LOVE ABOUT IT, AND HOW DID IT MAKE YOU FEEL?

Passion is not reserved for our dream jobs alone. We can also experience passion in the things we do for fun. An average working day is eight hours, and another eight hours are spent sleeping. That leaves us a whole eight hours to do whatever we please. We may still have our day-to-day commitments, but in those eight hours, there is still time to spend as we choose. In fact, it should be a priority to use some of that time to do what fuels our hearts and feeds our souls.

The trouble with 21st-century living is that life is full of distractions, and those eight hours can pass by in the blink of an eye. They say that time flies when you are having fun, but are we really having fun, or are we using modern distractions to fill the emptiness within? Are we using digital entertainment to pass the time, to stop us from thinking about how unfulfilled we are, or does it truly feed our joy and bring us a sense of peace? When we were young, we didn't have these modern distractions, and we found ways to entertain ourselves that often became our passions. Our boredom forced us to venture out and try new things.

I have always been a very girly-girl, and one of my favourite pastimes was doing hair. I dreamed of having long, beautiful locks like my sisters so I could brush and plait it, which possibly has something to do with my love for hair, but I had to make do with my boyish haircut. I used anyone or anything with hair as my models, and I lived my little passionate existence. I clearly remember standing on the back of my auntie Claire's chair while putting curlers in her hair. Even when I was as young as three, I had already decided I wanted to be a hairstylist. I had passion, even then, and it grew as I did. I laugh when I look back at old photos and my hairstyles, and that includes those I inflicted on my poor sister and friends who I used as guinea pigs. They had to pay the price of my passion, but at least one of us was having fun.

I loved hairdressing because I could express my creativity, make people feel better about themselves, and build deep and meaningful relationships. My passion for hairdressing may have faded, but passion itself has not, as I still live life, expressing my creativity, helping people feel better about themselves, *and* building deep and meaningful relationships.

Cast your mind back to your favourite pastimes and hobbies – what did you love doing the most? What hobbies are still a part of your life? What did you grow out of and what naturally faded away due to the busyness of life? We are not only here to write a legacy and make peace with the past – we are here to reignite our inner-sparks. What we once loved may no longer fuel our souls, but we owe it to ourselves to seek out what we love and try new things until we discover what does. There is a whole world out there, and it is ours for the taking.

What did a successful life look like to you, and how has that changed?

The beauty of growing older is the wisdom that comes with each passing year. The more challenges we have to overcome, the more opportunities we have to gain wisdom. So, let's be grateful for the challenges as well as the good times because they teach us many lessons along the way. We may look at other people's happy lives and feel as if life has been unfair to us, but in actual fact, we have no idea what is going on in their hearts, minds, and souls, or whether they are truly happy, so we cannot compare our lives with theirs.

When we are young, our dreams and visions of success tend to be measured by what we can attain on a material level, but with wisdom, we realise that the true treasures of life are people and joyful experiences, and success becomes about living a happy, healthy, and peaceful life with the people we love. That is not to say that we no longer appreciate having lovely homes, nice cars, exotic holidays, and all those other things that make life enjoyable, but we come to know that they are secondary to health, happiness, and wellbeing.

Success on a worldly level was important to me as a young woman. Being a successful business owner in my early twenties had its benefits, as I was still living with my parents and was able to splurge on material possessions to treat my friends and family to expensive weekends away without any concern for the future. As I said earlier, at that time, I had no desire to get married or have a family, so I was a free agent. I was living a great life, and that is how I imagined my life would continue. My mum used to say, "One day you'll regret wasting your money, and you'll wish you'd saved it," but I knew, deep down, that I wouldn't. I wanted to truly live and experience life, and that was what I was doing. I wasn't the partying type, but I did love my luxury weekends away as well as my holidays abroad every two or three months. I was living my idea of a successful life, but as I matured, so did my dreams. When I eventually settled down, got married, and started a family, I was happy to leave that life behind.

The pinnacle of success in my eyes is my personal freedom; freedom to live, being my true self. Over and above the essentials of life – such as a warm home, food, and a bed to sleep in – success is living life with meaning, purpose, happiness, good health, energy, and joy. Material wealth doesn't come into it for me, personally, but that doesn't make it wrong. I welcome it, but I don't use it to measure success. As you bring your youthful ideas about success to mind, think about where those ideas came from. Did they come from your heart, from others, or were they about becoming a success in the hope of impressing others? Think about what you hoped to gain from becoming successful and how your ideas have changed.

How did you feel about your self-image, and how has that changed now that you are older?

Have you ever sat with an older person as they looked through old photos, remarking how beautiful or handsome they once were? Well, I have. I also used to marvel at their self-confidence because I had none, but just a few years ago, I was flicking through some old photos, and I found one of myself from 20 years ago, and I looked beautiful. I was completely shocked as I had mostly seen myself as ugly. I turned to my kids and said, "Look at how beautiful I used to be."

At that moment, I realised I had become one of those older people. It was not that they were super-confident at all – they simply recognised that they were once young and attractive. They were on the outside looking in and just stating a fact. I was beautiful, and the evidence was there in full colour, yet I had wasted so much of my life putting myself through hell and struggling with my self-image issues. At that time, I was still carrying the old conditioning of being *the ugly sister* with me, but suddenly, I saw things as they really were. Then, I imagined myself 20 years on, looking at photos of myself today, saying the same thing, and something shifted within me. I wondered: *If I thought I was ugly 20 years ago, and I clearly wasn't, perhaps I'm not ugly now.*

What we were led to believe – or how we believed we looked as children – can become so tightly woven into our subconscious that we don't realise it is an inaccurate reflection of who we are. My self-image was distorted by my feelings of never feeling beautiful enough or good enough as a child, which affected me for the majority of my life. As I mentioned earlier in the book, the fact that my mum called herself ugly daily and being told I was my mum's double didn't help. On top of feeling ugly, I also had guilt because I knew I was fortunate for having a fully working face and body. I could see, hear, speak, eat, smell, and smile, so I hated myself for even caring what I looked like and for being so shallow. No matter how I looked, I couldn't shift the image I had of myself.

Thankfully, through inner-work, self-awareness, and a little wisdom, I was able to free myself from my attachment to the ugly label. I began to love and accept myself and simply be me, regardless of how I looked. I stopped seeking validation or acceptance from others in order to feel loved. I was free.

How did you see yourself when you were young, and how did it affect you? Were you happy about the way you looked then, and how does that compare to how you see yourself now? As you write your story, be honest and open with yourself and your family. Not only will it begin to free you from your old conditioning, but it will also encourage your family to do the same. The truth is that true beauty comes from within, and we all know it.

WHAT KIND OF FRIENDS DID YOU HAVE, AND WHAT INFLUENCE DID THEY HAVE ON YOU?

Friendships play a big part at any age or stage of life, but especially in the early years. I read somewhere that adolescents value the opinion of and listen to the advice of their peers over their parents or other adults. This came as no surprise to me, but it did scare me a little because if this is the case, it is important to know who our children are spending time with. As parents, we can lay the foundations for our children, but as they grow, we simply have to trust that they have enough sense to do the right thing and make the right choices for themselves.

One bad decision can change the whole trajectory of their lives, so who they spend time with matters, but let's face it – there is no such thing as good kids or bad kids. There are only happy and secure kids or unhappy and lost kids. They aren't bad, they are perhaps troubled or have had a difficult childhood that might have led them to make some bad choices.

I believe that, as adult human beings, we tend to gravitate towards people who think like we think and like things we like. Being with like-minded people makes us feel more comfortable and at ease with being ourselves, but in the adolescent stage, rebellion sets in, and we begin to test our boundaries as we get curious and explore the diversities of life on our own. Our curiosity and uncertainty about who we are can lead us down dangerous paths or lead us to make foolish decisions that can jeopardise our futures.

A few years ago, I watched a heartbreaking documentary about a 17-year-old boy who ruined the lives of two families, all because of one bad decision. One night, when he and his friends were alone at his house, they raided the family's liquor cabinet and drank until they were completely drunk out of their minds, but it didn't end there. This boy thought it would be fun to take his parents' car for a spin. While on this spin, he crashed into the car of a family on their way home from an evening out, instantly killing the mother and two of her children. The father and one child survived the crash, but needless to say, their lives were torn apart. This was not a bad boy, but he made a bad decision. Most of us made some poor choices growing up, but this poor boy lost a bright and carefree future, his freedom, his inner-peace, and essentially a normal life, all because of one bad decision.

I was fortunate enough to grow up surrounded by friends who truly cared about me, and most of us remain friends 30 years later. The dynamics have changed, but our loyalty and commitment to each other remain the same. I can honestly say that their presence in my life has been invaluable.

WHO WERE YOUR GREATEST ROLE MODELS, AND HOW DID THEY INFLUENCE YOUR LIFE?

In today's world, with the power of technology, access to the world's wisest, wonderful, and influential people is unlimited. This was not the case just a generation ago when we only had access to family and those within our immediate community who could enrich our lives with wisdom and positive energy. There were, of course, TV and music celebrities, movie stars, and even authors who influenced us but they were not as easily accessible to us as they are today.

When we were small children, our parents were our world, and everything they said or did had some impact on our lives, but as we grew up and developed our characters, we began to seek other influences. These influences or role models may be older siblings, aunties, uncles, family friends, or grandparents. Mine was my auntie, Claire.

She was a family friend who used to babysit us, but I only remember her as Auntie Claire. As my parents were far from their family homes, my grandmothers were not a part of my life, so I think I subconsciously adopted Auntie Claire as my grandmother.

So many people I have met over the years had deep bonds with their grandparents, and that is what I had with her. She meant the world to me, was my go-to person, and whatever she said was gold. I believed she could see the real me. In fact, she was the only person who made me feel I was of true worth.

Every one of us is a role model to the people around us, whether or not we are aware of it. The question is whether we are positive or negative ones. We can be either drains or radiators, meaning that we can either drain the joy and enthusiasm out of others or radiate warmth and light to nourish them, but lives can be influenced by both. Understanding this helps us be aware of the energy we emit to help us become the kind of people for which we want to be remembered. As you recall the good role models in your life, ask yourself why they influenced you the way they did. What was it about them that you admired, and what life lessons did they teach you through their words and actions? Notice the energy you presently emit and decide what kind of role model you want to be. It is never too late to shine.

WHAT WERE YOU LIKE AS A TEENAGER? WHAT ADVICE WOULD YOU GIVE TO YOUR YOUNGER SELF?

If only we knew then what we know now, how different would our lives have been? Then again, everything happened exactly as it was meant to, which was essential for our personal evolution and growth.

Life is a classroom, and as we progress, we can become wiser. We can enjoy what life has to teach us, or we can spend our time complaining about it. Either way, we are all in the same class, even if we have differing levels of understanding. There are no grades – we simply get out what we put in. The more we experience, the more wisdom we can gain, depending on whether we decide to be victims or victors in life.

My only real regret in life is how I behaved toward my mum as a teen because she didn't deserve the abuse that I threw at her. I treated her like the enemy most of the time, and she reacted defensively. As a mother to teens and with all the research and training I have done over the years concerning mind management and emotional wellbeing, I make a conscious effort not to react to my children's hormonal outbursts, though I am not always successful. I remind myself of how badly I treated my mum at that age, and it helps me to realise that they are not monsters – they are simply adjusting to life as they transition into adulthood.

Parenting growing children is not easy for us, either, because our once sweet little children who used to rely on us for everything are now unrecognisable. Of course, we are happy that our children are growing up and becoming increasingly more independent; nevertheless, we can feel pushed out and unwanted, which can hurt.

I know this is not the case for everyone, but it certainly was for me, due to my old conditioning, my unresolved issues, and my need for love and validation from others, and I unwittingly used my children to fill the emptiness within me when it was not their responsibility to do so; it was mine. I was completely unaware of the deep-rooted conditioning within myself that was at the core of all my suffering.

If I could go back to give my teenage-self advice, I would say, "Deep down, you know Mum loves you, and she is on your team. Everything she says and does is because she believes it is the best for you. She may make mistakes, but it is not easy for her, either. You were once her little girl, and she now has to adjust to the new, independent you, so treat her with more kindness and love and be patient with her."

How well did you manage your emotions as a teenager, and how did you feel about your transition into adulthood?

I can only speak for myself here as we are all so diverse, but at the core, I have not changed that much since I was a teen. What *has* grown exponentially over the years is the ability to manage my emotions. I am in no way a master of my emotions yet, but as I consistently say, we are all works in progress, so each step I take in the right direction is a success in my eyes.

I did get lost for a few years when I hit midlife, but through looking within, I was able to find and rescue myself from the fog. Middle-age and the teenage years are both emotionally challenging times of change, but if you are fortunate enough, you will get to experience both and the joy of transitioning through each period. Whether life has been hard on you or you have lived a blissfully happy life so far, you have lived and made it through alive, so simply being here should be a celebration. Not everyone has made it this far, so let's be grateful for every moment we do have and enjoy this time.

When I was young, I was an introvert, deep, insecure, very emotional, and highly sensitive. I hid my emotions which only caused me more internal pain. When I opened up and was myself, I seemed to scare people away, so instead of becoming the master of my emotions, I became a master of disguise.

To some extent, a lot of teenage girls probably do the same, trying to identify themselves through the clothes they wear or their hair and make-up, but these are just masks to hide their insecurities with the hope of gaining external validation.

When I left the comfort of school at 16, I remember being terrified of growing up and having to step into the unknown and face the world. As excited as I was to begin following my dream of becoming a hairdresser, I can still remember being scared of taking the step from a carefree child to an adult. However, once I set off on my new path, I felt free to be myself and poured all the love I had within me into my work, and it showed.

Managing our emotions at any age is no easy feat. As we get older, we expect our emotions to take care of themselves naturally, but of course, that is not the case. Emotional wellbeing needs to be taught – or at least guided – which is why I do what I do. There is such a stigma attached to being open and honest about our emotions, but if we were all more open and honest about how we feel, we would realise that we are more alike than different. We would realise that we are not alone in our emotional challenges which would enable us to build deeper connections.

As a teen, how did the transition to adulthood affect you emotionally? Were you excited to grow up or were you apprehensive about the future? Did you express your feelings to others or did you keep them to yourself? None of us is exempt from emotional challenges as they are a part of the human experience; we simply have to decide whether to be their masters or their slaves.

How did you behave at school, and was it different from the way you behaved at home?

Most of us have a public persona and a private one reserved for friends and family, as very few of us dare to be our true selves with everyone. This does not mean that we are necessarily false – it means that we are well-mannered. The truth is that not everyone with whom we interact is that interested in who we are. People simply want us to be kind in our interactions with them.

I am an advocate for being open and being our true selves, but spilling our guts out to everyone we meet is perhaps a little excessive – which is ironic as I am spilling mine out onto these pages.

When we are small children, we do not give any thought to what others think of us. We could kick and scream in public and be completely unaware of the scenes we cause while our parents look frantically around, wondering what people think as they try to hide in shame. Statements such as, "Everyone's looking at you," "You're causing a scene," or "You're embarrassing yourself," taught us to mask our true emotions in front of others from a young age. We came to believe it shameful to express our fears and frustrations freely, and we carried these beliefs into our teens and beyond. At school, we learn that the more compliant we are, the easier our lives are. Keeping quiet without questioning what we learnt was the key to being a "good" student. Rarely did our teachers take a personal interest in us unless we were exceptional students or particularly disruptive or troubled. We spent hours at school every day, conforming to social conditioning, essentially suppressing our true nature, holding in our emotions, and shielding our true selves from the world. It is not surprising that we came home to our parents ablaze with frustration – home was a safe space for us to vent, and only those we felt truly safe with saw the real us, warts and all. The people in our lives who deserved the best parts of us often got the worst.

Sadly, we carry a lot of this conditioning into adulthood and keep our true selves hidden deep within. I was in my forties before the light of my true self awakened within me. The big-hearted, highly sensitive little girl in me came bursting out with joy and enthusiasm when the barriers could no longer contain me. When I started opening up, being and sharing my true self with the people within my reach, they also began opening up to me. We were all hiding, scared to look deep within for fear of what we might find – fear of not being loved and accepted for who we *really* are – but to be loved for who we are, we first have to *be* our true selves.

I was a "good" kid in school, and got through fairly unnoticed, conforming to the social norms and suppressing my true nature, but I was happy because I had my friends with me. What kind of student were you? Did you question authority and make waves, or did you dim your light? As you share your stories, bring your emotions to mind and think about why you behaved the way you did.

HOW DID YOU WANT TO BE PERCEIVED BY OTHERS, AND WHY?

We all have an idea of how we want to be perceived by others, and it is very personal to each of us. When we are children, we imagine ourselves becoming superheroes, princesses, pop stars, and the like and being seen as special, but as we grow and develop, our ideas also evolve.

I believe that we are all born with passions, gifts, talents, likes, and dislikes for a reason. Our intuition (aka our gut feelings, inner voices or deep knowing) is our true guide in life, but as we grow up, we can get so caught up with what is going on in the world that we begin to care more about how we are seen by others and less about how we feel.

Once we begin to look within instead of looking around and listen to our inner voices, we will be led in the right direction, which will bring meaning and joy to our lives. The lesson here is to trust your gut and listen to your inner voice, and your life will flow with greater ease.

When I was a child, I didn't want to be seen at all. I wanted to blend in with everyone else. When we lived in the city, my sisters and I were just normal kids, but when we moved to a picturesque town in Scotland, we were suddenly foreigners. I had never given any thought to my race or colour as we were always surrounded by different cultures, so the transition to living in a quiet little town was quite a shock to the system. I found myself hiding my brown skin and wearing long sleeves even on the hottest of days so my skin wouldn't get any darker. The people were lovely and friendly, but like everywhere in the world, there were those few who had to make us feel different. We were bullied for being of mixed race, and when I was about eight or nine, my sisters and I found our names scribbled on a wall describing us as sluts. I had no idea what that meant, and why would I? So, my life became about *not* being seen and *not* being singled out, and I carried that with me for most of my life.

It was only when I began my mission to help people gain more love and light and find themselves that I was brave enough to stand up and really be seen. My life's purpose depended on it. I had to get out of my own way, stand out, and speak up. Was it easy? No, it was terrifying, but I knew that if I wanted to make a difference in the lives of others, I had to step out of my comfort zone. My soul had a calling; therefore, I had to push my fear of being seen aside and listen to that inner voice. I had to lead by example!

GROWING UP, WERE YOUR LIFE CHOICES INFLUENCED BY OTHERS, OR WERE YOU SELF-DRIVEN AND SELF-MOTIVATED?

Regardless of whether we are influenced by others or not, we ultimately decide which paths to take. We may have made excuses, saying that we have no choice, but let's be honest – most of the time, we had a choice, we simply chose to give in or make wrong choices, perhaps to be accepted by others. Deep down, we knew what was right for us, but at times, we ignored our inner voice and simply chose to go against it. As teens, we thought we were so grown up, believed we knew it all, and began to question the boundaries our parents had set by fighting back on many aspects. We seemed to think that they were trying to control us or be the killjoys in our lives. I see it in my kids now, and I remember doing the same with my mum, but most of what I did was to purposefully hurt my poor mum.

Even though I did follow the crowd to some extent, I was not heavily influenced by what others thought of me or what they did. At 15, most of my friends smoked, but because my parents smoked and I hated it, I had no interest in starting smoking. I was still sucking my thumb at that time, though I was unashamed of it, so when my friends hid under the bridge, smoking, I was happily in their company with my thumb – and not a cigarette – firmly planted in my mouth. When I got home, my mum smelled the smoke on me and accused me of smoking. Of course, I denied it, but she never believed me, and I always got into trouble for it. This happened a few times until I had had enough of being punished for something I did not do, and I decided I would start smoking just to spite my mum. I was already being punished for it, so I thought that I might as well do the crime. Overall, though, I was pretty much a good little Catholic girl most of the time. The fear of hell and damnation kept me in check, and the guilt was too much of a burden for me to carry, which kept me on the straight and narrow. It may have brought a whole other set of challenges, but going way off track was not one of them. Between fearing the wrath of my mum and the wrath of God, I was pretty safe where I was.

You may have been immune to outside influence, too. Nevertheless, whether we like it or not, whether we are conscious of it or not, we are influenced in some way by the people around us. When we are surrounded by passionate and enthusiastic people, it rubs off on us. Alternately, if we spend time with negative people, that, too, rubs off, so we have to be careful who we spend our time with, as well as how we act and behave ourselves.

Our children absorb our energy, be it good or not so good, so if we want our children to have more joy and enthusiasm for life, the best way to help them is for us to *be* the people we wish our children to become.

WHAT WAS YOUR FIRST PAID JOB, HOW MUCH DID YOU GET PAID, AND HOW DID YOU FEEL ABOUT WORKING?

As parents, it is not only our job to take care of our children's physical and emotional needs, but it is also our duty to prepare them for life and teach them self-reliance. The best way to do this is to teach them by example, so they will know the value of hard work.

You may not agree with me, but I believe that so many from our generation seem to have the idea that we should provide for our kids, not only for now but also for the future. We want them to live better lives than we have, which is only natural, but by giving our kids *everything* they want or need, we compromise their personal growth. Just as we cannot eat to help them feel physically nourished, we cannot do the work for them to give them a sense of accomplishment. They are responsible for their lives, and the sooner we give them responsibility, the sooner they will learn. If not, what might happen when it is time for them to leave the nest? Will they expect life to provide them with all they need and desire? How will they feel when they do not get what they want? As much as we want to show our children how much we love them by giving them what they want, we are actually setting them up for disappointment. The harsh reality is that one day, we will not be around to support them emotionally, physically, or financially, and the best thing we can do for them now is to teach them self-reliance by *not* giving them what they want. They will soon realise that to get what they want in life, they have to work for it, and they will come to understand the value of hard work, roll up their sleeves, and get on with it. As well as bringing them financial gain, they will also feel a great sense of self-worth and accomplishment from working. Now, how could we possibly deny them that?

I grew up in a home where we all worked together as a family to help out in the restaurant. Work was a part of my daily life, and I am now truly grateful for that. At the time, however, I believed my mum was a tyrant for making me do the housework, and I thought of work as a cruel punishment. Of course, as an adult, and especially as a parent, I now truly appreciate my mum's insistence and unrelenting persistence when it came to making me work. With all of the resistance I put up, my mum could have easily given in, but thankfully, her determination to prepare my sisters and me for the future paid off. If she had let me have my way, I would have probably loved her more, and she knew that, but she understood that her role as a mother wasn't about being loved but preparing us for adulthood.

I can now see how much love and energy my mum put into being a mother, and I am grateful that she loved me enough *not* to give me everything I wanted. Whatever my sisters and I wanted, we had to earn it by working in our restaurant or at our part-time jobs. Because work is such an essential part of life, my parents made sure we were well-prepared for the future.

As you recount your experience concerning your first paid job, think about how you felt when you received your wage at the end of the week and what you used to do with your earnings. What was your attitude towards work then?

WHAT ARE SOME OF THE JOBS YOU HAD? WHICH ONES DID YOU LOVE, WHICH DID YOU HATE, AND WHY?

Some people know what they want at a young age and spend their whole lives pursuing it, mastering their crafts along the way. Others leave school and go straight into a job they spend the rest of their lives doing that doesn't really excite them, but they are happy enough and content in life, so they stay. Yet others long for a life with a job they love, but their lack of self-confidence or fear holds them back, so they settle for less and spend their lives wishing how things could have been different. In their desperation to end the monotony of their daily working lives, they yearn for early retirement, essentially wishing their lives away. Perhaps they feel powerless over their circumstances but fail to realise they are missing out on living each day as they wait for a future event to make them happy. This makes me so sad because they believe that their time has passed, but it is never too late.

Have you ever said to yourself things such as *I'll be happy when I can retire; I'll be happy when I lose weight; I'll be happy when I get that promotion; I'll be happy when I meet the right person?* What about now? How many days,

141

months, or years are we prepared to waste waiting? The harsh but true reality is that our days on this earth are numbered, so should we waste them waiting for happiness to appear in our lives, or are we ready to take back control of our lives and start being happy today?

We don't have to have a great life's purpose when it comes to our working lives, but we were each born with a longing, a special gift or unique talent, and we simply have to listen carefully and do what lights up our souls without caring about other people's opinions or allowing our fears to hold us back. We are the only ones who know what makes our hearts sing, so not only do we have to take the time to be still and truly listen, we also have to encourage our children to do the same when making their life choices. Work doesn't have to be work – it can be living our days joyfully, doing what we love with the bonus of getting paid for it, but in order to do what we love, we must step up and out of our comfort zones, own our passions, gifts, or talents, and take action. Our dream jobs will not miraculously turn up in our lives – we need to make it happen.

I have spent my life pursuing my dreams, and more often than not, I hit the mark because I was unwavering in that pursuit. When I did what I loved doing, I was a great success, and when I didn't, I wasn't. We cannot fail at anything we do with love, so we can either remain failures or learn to love what we do. An example of this is that I used to hate cooking because my food always tasted horrible, especially when compared to anything my parents had cooked. Of course, it did. My dad was an incredibly talented and passionate chef, and my mum was a typical Italian mamma whose food was beyond delicious. Once I decided to make an effort and actually learn how to cook properly, by watching and helping my parents cook, I developed a different attitude towards cooking, and I started to do it with more love – you could literally taste the love in my food. We all love a home-cooked meal because *love* is the main ingredient. That is the same with anything else we do in life, too. When we put passion and love into our work, we cannot fail.

We may not create an abundance of wealth, but we can absolutely create an abundant life.

My favourite job, hands down, was being a full-time mum to my babies, and even though I didn't get paid, it gave me the greatest rewards because I lived each day, doing what I loved. Being here, writing this book, may come second to motherhood, but it, too, is not work. It is living each day with passion and doing what I love with a joyful heart.

How aware were you of your health, diet, and wellbeing as a young person? How did you feel about your body, and how did you treat your body?

If only we knew then what we know now, perhaps our lives and health would be different. Would we have made better choices? If we had known the effects what we ate and drank had on our bodies, would we have been so carefree?

This may sound weird, but I was "lucky enough to have tasted death" in my early twenties. It was the wakeup call I needed to kick my backside into gear and get my health in order. When we are young, we think we are invincible for some reason, and the last thing most of us think about is how our bodies will look and feel 30-, 40-, or 50-plus years down the line, but what we do not realise is that life passes by in an instant, and before we know it, we find ourselves in middle-age and quite frankly, not always much wiser when it comes to our health.

When we are young, many of us might have been careful about what we ate because we were concerned about our looks, but those of us who were healthy took our good health for granted. We had no idea of what physical challenges were and were oblivious to the effects of food on our bodies other than what made us fat. Who ever heard of health foods then? We also made the mistake of believing that thin equates to being healthy, but that certainly was not the case then, and it is not now.

I have never been overweight as such, but I was most certainly unhealthy. In my ignorance as a teen, I was so focused on my weight that I dieted, abusing my body with meal replacement shakes and the like. There was a product on the market, cubes of delicious fudge, that were supposed to fill you up and were eaten instead of a meal to avoid weight gain, and my friend and I used to eat the whole box because we were so hungry. Between diets, I would stuff my face with my dad's delicious Chinese food that was difficult to resist, and eat all the crisps, sweets, and chocolate that I could get my hands on. My carefree attitude towards my diet took its toll on my body, and along with the smoking, I ended up with chronic asthma which eventually took over my life.

I now see what happened as a blessing because my near-death experience ultimately saved me from a lifetime of suffering. I had to put in the work to overhaul my life. It was not easy by any means, but it was worth all the effort and hard work. I had no idea that what I was putting into my system was doing so much damage. I thought asthma was something that just happened to me, but once I had cleaned up my diet, started eating good, clean, healthy foods, retrained my breathing, and started to take care of my health, radical changes took place. Twenty-five years on and I am fitter and healthier now than I was in my twenties, and I have never looked back.

WHAT ADVICE WOULD YOU GIVE YOUR YOUNGER SELF CONCERNING HEALTH AND FUTURE WELLBEING?

Five years ago, while chatting to my sister in her bar in Italy, a young man walked in, ordered a cola and a brioche, scoffed them down in two minutes flat, and promptly ordered round two. I stood beside him, my eyes welling up with tears as I was so concerned for his health. I had to hold myself back from taking him gently by the arms, looking him straight in the eyes, and telling him that one was enough. The poor boy was oblivious to the fact that a stranger was more concerned for his wellbeing than he. I wanted to ask whether he was trying to fill his belly or an emptiness within his heart, but even if I had, I'm sure he wouldn't have known the answer.

Even though I'd never been overweight, both of my sisters were. I love them so much, and watching them struggle daily with it was heartbreaking for me. They tried every diet and bought all the keep fit videos and gadgets at the time, but nothing worked. I also felt guilty because I was a normal weight and they weren't, even though we ate the same things, so our lives revolved around obsessing about our weight – not our health, but our weight. Pretty much everyone else we knew was the same, and to be honest, the world hasn't really changed much except that now we now call it being health-conscious; it is still all about body and image consciousness.

If I could talk to my teenage self, I would say, "Be aware of what you put into your body because it will determine your health, energy, and beauty for the years ahead. Choose wisely. Eat clean, fresh, natural foods that will nourish you. This body must last you a lifetime, so treat it lovingly. Focus on eating for your health and what makes your body feel good, not what makes it look good. If you do that, you won't ever have to diet. Simply eat consciously and not mindlessly, move more and be kind to yourself. I promise that you will thank me for this advice one day."

As parents, we want our children to take good care of their health and wellbeing and don't make the same mistakes as us, but we can only encourage, educate, and set an example of living a healthy lifestyle. Ultimately, they are responsible for their health, just as we were and still are. Making excuses, blaming, and complaining about the state of our health, even telling ourselves blatant untruths, will not change our realities. Only being honest with ourselves, deciding we deserve better, and making the necessary changes will improve our health and wellbeing – it is all in our hands.

WHO WERE YOUR IDOLS, AND WHAT WAS IT ABOUT THEM THAT MADE YOU LOVE THEM OR WANT TO BE LIKE THEM?

One thing that will never change is the teen idol phase. Everyone was once besotted by some public persona in their teens, and it was a magical time. I can only speak for myself here, but I used to daydream about meeting Duran Duran. John Taylor would take one look at me and fall instantly in love. These wonderful, far-fetched dreams felt truly possible in my young eyes, as I imagined a future full of wonder and possibilities. To be honest, I have come full circle because I can again see a life of wonder and endless possibilities, but John Taylor is no longer the man of my dreams.

I believe that ageing is accelerated by losing the ability to dream new dreams and visualise a bright new future. Our energy becomes stagnant and blocks the natural flow of abundance into our lives because we lose our carefree nature as we get caught up in life's daily challenges and allow it to steal our dreams and crush our joyful spirits. Instead of seeing the joy and enthusiasm in others as an inspiration, they are reminders of what we failed to achieve in our lives. The beauty of getting older is, however, the wisdom that comes from living life. As we grow in knowledge and experience, we also grow in depth, and in time, perhaps in width a little, too. Nevertheless, we still have so much to learn about who we are and also about life, which, in itself, gives our lives meaning and purpose. Life is a journey of growth and personal evolution, and no matter what age we are, there is always space to dream big and live with hopeful hearts. The best of life is far from over, and perhaps the best is yet to come. We may be older in years, but who says we can't retain or regain our youthful ideas about life? Life ends when we take our final breaths, but until that day comes, we still have that source of life pumping through our veins, so dream new dreams and open your heart, mind, and soul to a bright new future.

As you reminisce and remember your teen idols and teenage dreams, let them ignite that spark of enthusiasm back in your heart. Life is too short to waste time mourning lives we once had. The beauty of dreaming is that there are no limits to what our minds can create. We all too often dream up problems and create fears in our minds that do not serve us, so instead, let's choose positive and exciting thoughts and dreams to create bright and beautiful futures, overflowing with an abundance of love, light, laughter, and joy.

WHAT DID YOU LIKE AND DISLIKE ABOUT SCHOOL? IS THERE SOMETHING YOU WISH YOU'D HAD THE OPPORTUNITY TO LEARN DURING YOUR SCHOOL YEARS?

As much as I know how important school was and still is, I always wonder how much of what we learnt was of any use to us in later life. Don't get me wrong – there is so much value in school, but do children leave school any wiser than when they started? They may have memorised many facts and figures, but how many important life lessons have they learnt? Are they prepared to face the challenges of life and become self-reliant emotionally, physically, and mentally? They are being taught to fill their minds, but can they manage their minds? I understand that parents have to play their part, but with the school curriculum as it stands, are our children left with sufficient headspace to take in other valuable life lessons? I wish I was taught these life lessons at school. In fact, I strongly believe that awareness and mind management should be a part of the main curriculum in all schools for all ages as it is of paramount importance in all areas of life.

When I decided to study hairdressing, one of my friends asked me why I did not want to stay on in school to get a better education. She said to me, "You're quite clever and could be more than just a hairdresser, you know." I know she meant well, but she did not understand my passion because she did not know what she wanted in life. To her, school was about getting good grades and being top of the class, but that meant absolutely nothing to me. I enjoyed school, but getting good grades and comparing myself with others never even crossed my mind. I did well in the subjects I enjoyed and not quite as well in the ones I did not. I was happy with that and never felt any pressure to do better. As my parents were both foreign, neither of them could help my sisters and me with our homework, so we just got on with it. When we got good grades, it was all our doing, which gave us a sense of achievement.

I loved school as I was happy being with my friends, but I felt no need to prove anything to myself or anyone else. I knew what I wanted to do in life, and nothing anyone could have said or done would have come between me and my dreams. Even now, when I know what I want to do, I simply do all I can to make it happen, and if it is meant to be, it will be. I do not power through, hoping it will happen – I make it happen.

What career path did you take, and how did it lead you to where you are today?

I was one of the lucky ones who knew exactly what I wanted to do with my life. It wasn't a decision I made, I just couldn't imagine myself doing anything else, so I naturally followed my heart. Imagine if we were taught to quieten our overthinking minds, to become still enough to listen to our inner voices,–how wonderful it would be! Everyone would simply follow their heart to do what comes naturally. Unfortunately, some young people can get sucked into other people's ideas about what success looks like, and they are led down paths to careers they *think* will bring them success only to find that it doesn't make them happy.

If we have to spend so much of our lives working, whether paid or unpaid, we must follow our hearts and do what brings us joy. Our worth should not be based on what we do for a living but on how joyful we are and how passionate we are about our work. Is a full-time parent worth less than a CEO? Is a council worker worth less than a doctor? Absolutely not; we are of equal worth, yet social conditioning can lead us to believe that we should be more to be of worth. We may have more drive, energy, and passion for a certain type of work, but that doesn't make us more valuable than someone else.

I was a full-time mum for many years. One day, I met someone I had not seen for years, and she asked me what I was up to. I told her that I was a full-time mum, and she replied, "What? You don't work?" I explained to her that being a full-time mum *was* my work, and I told her how much I loved it. Yes, I had to do without the luxuries of life and live frugally, but I had never been happier. As she had known me years earlier as a successful business owner, she could not comprehend why I would give it all up, "just to be a mum".

As we grow and evolve, our priorities change – it is a natural part of life. My time as a full-time mum was magical for me, and I do not regret it. I did struggle to find my feet and get back into the "real world", but the challenge itself gave me the experience I needed to enable me to help others find their feet, too. It was all part of the universe's plan for me.

As you answer this question, think about why you took your particular path and how you felt at the time. Did you follow your heart, or did you take the advice of others? Did it ultimately lead you to find your passion or lead you away from it?

WHO, OTHER THAN YOUR PARENTS, TAUGHT YOU VALUABLE LIFE LESSONS AND HOW HAVE THOSE LESSONS HELPED YOU?

We were all influenced by the people by which we are surrounded. Whether they supported us in our personal growth or played a significant role in our downfall, they each taught us valuable lessons. Those who played their part in our shortcomings taught us who and what we *did not* want to be, and those who inspired us were able to shine a light on our paths forward. We are who we are today due to our past experiences, which includes the various people who have crossed our paths. Ultimately, though, we decided who we would become.

One of my friends has a severely disabled child, and for the past 20 years or so, she has been his full-time caregiver, as well as a mother to her other two children. I cannot even begin to understand the struggles she faces and the multiple challenges, day after day, month after month, and year after year. I truly admire her physical and emotional strength. No matter what is going on in her life, she continues to laugh and smile. I often wonder if I would have been so strong under the same circumstances; my life, in comparison, has been a piece of cake. I truly admire her and am grateful for her inspiration.

When I was a hairdresser some 20 years ago, I was fortunate to have many wise and wonderful ladies who came to the salon on a weekly basis and taught me so much. They were like my surrogate grandmothers, dishing out life advice, telling me to live life the way I choose, and to listen to my heart instead of other people because life will pass in a blink of an eye. They would look in the mirror and tell me that they did not recognise the old face staring back at them as they still felt like 20-year-olds inside. Their words of wisdom rang deep within me, and I could feel their love through those words. Leaving my ladies was the hardest part of selling the business and moving away, but they had taught me well and were happy for me when we said our goodbyes. Not many of them are alive now, but I am grateful for the gift of their life experiences which have served me well.

Those that have gone before you have so much to teach you, just as this work and your life's experiences will serve your children and grandchildren. They, too, will face challenges and heartache, but your words and loving light will help them through their darkest times, and your written legacy will be a source of love and strength for them.

IF YOU COULD PRESS THE RESET BUTTON ON YOUR LIFE, WHAT WOULD YOU PUT MORE LOVE AND ENERGY INTO THIS TIME AROUND? WHAT ELSE WOULD YOU DO DIFFERENTLY?

I believe that it is never too late to press the reset button in life. We cannot go back and relive the past, but we can draw a line in the sand and start afresh. It is about clearing our minds of all the old limiting beliefs that we have carried around that have not served us. This releases us to take on what serves us best to set off down a new path. The truth is that our time is limited. Once we come to accept the reality of our mortality, we will no longer sit around, waiting for life to change and start truly living each day fully. Now is our chance to live, not yesterday, not tomorrow – this very moment. When we know that tomorrow is not guaranteed, why would we waste today? It may be scary to take a new path, especially later in life, but would you rather spend your life pursuing your dreams or burying them? When I get to the end of my life, I want to be able to say that I truly lived. Even if I had failed, I would be at peace, knowing that I gave life my best shot and left no stone unturned.

As you go through this book and retrace your steps, you will begin to understand a little more about who you are, what you want, and why you may have steered off course, not to blame, but to understand where you started to doubt yourself, lose faith in yourself, and your ability to live freely, being who you are. Let this encourage you to make the changes you want to make.

We are told to leave the past behind us, but if we lost ourselves in that past, it makes sense to go back to find ourselves again. If we lose our keys while out shopping, what would be the point in looking for them at home? If we are looking for something we never had, such as self-worth, then we can seek to create it, but if we are seeking that which we have lost, it is essential to retrace our steps in order to find it.

I have pressed the reset button three times in my life. First, when I nearly died as a result of asthma; second, when I gave up my successful business and moved to Italy; and finally, when I decided I was not ready to give up on my life due to depression. I can say, hand on heart, that I would not be here if I had not pressed that button. Remember that you may not always be able to change the circumstances in which you find yourself, but we have the power in our own hands to press that button and change course.

WHAT DO YOU LIKE ABOUT YOURSELF NOW, AFTER HAVING LIVED A GOOD PART OF YOUR LIFE? WHAT HAS CHANGED YOU FOR THE BETTER?

When we look in the mirror, we can see that our once youthful looks are now maturing. The signs of life now show on our faces and bodies. Perhaps we are a little wider, or our hair is a little thinner, greyer, or gone, but we are still alive. We have made it, and that is something of which to be proud. If I were offered the chance at a do-over, I wouldn't take it.

Whatever life has given us, we are better and stronger because of it, not in spite of it. We may have experienced tragedy, heartbreak, loss, and tremendous pain, but we have also made or attained little human beings who allowed us to know the greatest love of our lives, transforming us beyond measure. Has it been easy? Heck no, but I can't imagine that any one of us would live our lives over again without our children. Parenthood is the most challenging work we will ever do, and it pushes us to the limits physically, mentally, and emotionally, but we would not change it for the world. Parenthood changes us for the better.

What I like most about myself now is my courage. I also like the fact that I care less about what others think of me, especially when I realised that it stopped me from being me. Notice that I didn't say I do not care at all because that would not be entirely true – I just do not let that care hold me back. Before I started writing, I worried that people would think I was a fraud or not good enough to write books about life. I could hear them say, "Who does she think she is?" "What makes her the expert?" "Why should I listen to her?" The thing is that they were my thoughts – no one said these things to me. Even if they had, what did they know? I could protect myself from potential humiliation, but it was just that: *potential*. It would mean I was not true to myself if I let fear and doubt control me. I knew who I was, what was in my heart, and my intentions, so I faced my fears and doubts and followed my soul regardless.

If I wanted to make a difference in my life, I had to trust myself and my abilities. As a young woman, I lacked so much confidence and just wanted to be liked, but wisdom has taught me that I have to like me, and as long as I am good enough for me, then those that do not love me or appreciate me for who I am can say or think what they like.

HOW CLOSE IS YOUR LIFE TO THE DREAM LIFE
YOU IMAGINED YOU WOULD HAVE?

However old you are, your life is not your past. It is here, right now, and it is an ongoing journey. I know this sounds obvious, but how many of us think our lives are already over? When I hit middle-age, I slowly slipped into a dormant state without really noticing that I had. Even though I potentially had plenty more years ahead of me, I truly believed that my time to shine had passed.

I am not talking about shining externally, but about that inner-glow, the one I had once radiated as a young woman. I had slipped away from the passionate and enthusiastic person I used to be and felt that my options were limited. I had the energy, but fear and a lack of confidence held me back. I told myself stories such as…

You won't be able to do anything new now; you're too old.
You're too far behind to catch up with the rest of the world.
Everything is digital now, and you won't know what to do.
You're not good enough or clever enough to start afresh.

Those are just a few of the things I used to play over and over in my head until I slid down a spiral of sadness and negativity, mourning a life that was gone. It makes me sad now to think of how powerless I felt, but now that I look back, I realise I needed to hit rock bottom, to be broken open to see what was inside me.

I do all that I do and write because there are so many others that have been held prisoner by this same feeling of powerlessness over their lives. I may not be the best writer or have a magical way with words, but I know people, and I know the spirit, and it is important that I put that knowledge to use.

I used to wonder what on earth I was going to do with the rest of my life, and now I wonder if I will have the time to do all of the things I want to do and write all the books I want to write.

Your life may not have turned out exactly as you had hoped, but you simply have to trust that everything worked out perfectly for you to play your part in the symphony of life. We do not need to have a grand purpose in life to make a difference in the world; we simply have to be a source of love, hope, and strength for those who need us. The fact that you are here, writing your legacy for your family says so much about you, so be proud of yourself, and let your soul shine.

WHAT IS YOUR RELATIONSHIP WITH MONEY?

Money is an essential part of life, whether we like it or not. It is needed for what we now call the essentials. Having anything beyond what we need to survive is a personal choice; however, just as some people believe that what we do for a living has some bearing on our worth, some also believe the same about how much money we earn. We would all love to have our financial needs met and afford to buy everything that we want, but over and above what we need to survive comfortably, does money make us happy? Is that another story we have told ourselves? One thing I hear people say consistently through all ages and stages of life is that if they had more money, they would be happier, without question. My question is, does that mean we cannot be happy without money?

Our grandparents or great-grandparents probably lived with the bare of essentials, but did they wait for the day they came across great riches, or did they find joy in the simple things in life, like family, fresh air, walks in nature, picnics on the beach, swimming in the river on a hot day, or a Sunday roast? Do you really even know what it means to go hungry? You (and I) skip a meal and complain that you are starving, but we have no idea what starving feels like, and we are still not happy.

Although there is still vast inequality, life in the twenty-first century is the most comfortable and wealthy of all time. If we lived as we do now, even just 200 years ago, we would have been the richest across many lands. Despite this, we seem to be one of the unhappiest generations ever. Money most certainly makes life easier and more enjoyable, and our miseries easier to bear, but it does not create long-term happiness.

In today's world of comparison, we are becoming increasingly detached from one another and disconnected from the simplicities of life. We fill our lives with things with the hope of making ourselves happy, never stopping to consider that of which we are truly in need. In an attempt to feel complete and worthy, we fill up our homes and cupboards instead of filling our hearts and souls. Happiness comes from within, yet many of us seek it outside of ourselves through what we have and how we look to others. When it comes down to it, money may give us the freedom to go and do what we want in life, but it cannot make us happy.

As you go back through your life, you will come to realise that your happiest times were not related to what you had. Instead, it was the simple moments of love, kindness, and deep connection with others that brought us joy.

Question 61

WHAT BOOK, FILM, OR SONG LEFT AN IMPRESSION ON YOU?

Some of my greatest lessons have come to me through books and podcasts, so I understand the value of the written and spoken word. I do love music and movies for entertainment, but to be honest, spending hours and hours in front of the TV feels like a waste of quality time, unless, of course, I am cuddled up with my family, which is never a waste of time.

I picked up my first self-development book, *The Secrets of Abundant Happiness* by Adam J Jackson, about 25 years ago, and I was hooked. It made me see life through different lenses. The book's teachings fuelled me with enthusiasm and a wonder for life and kick-started my journey towards seeking out happiness and personal growth. As a child, I hated reading. I know! How strange to hear a writer say that she hated reading. I only read books when I absolutely had to and wondered why people would choose to read.

All of that turned on its head when I was in an airport and saw that book. With the Chinese character for happiness written on the cover, it stood out on the shelf, and that little book changed the whole trajectory of my life.

It was a lovely little fictional story, containing ten secrets that lit a spark, allowing me to see the power I had within me and awakening my curious mind. It taught me that my happiness was in my hands, and I could live the life of my dreams if I was willing to change my way of thinking.

Since then, I have been a "relentless seeker", seeking knowledge, wisdom, and truth about life, love, God, and the reason for why you and I are here. The books I read became my guides and life teachers. I learned from some and others not quite as much, but I grew, mind, body, and spirit.

When I became a mother, I focused on books about parenting to guide me to be the best mother I could for my children. I write now because I understand the power of books and the intimate relationship between author and reader to connect on a soul-level, and how that can propel the reader to a positive change.

Whether it was a book, film, or song that left an impression on you, recount how you felt about it, and how it touched your heart. What did it teach you about yourself or about life? Consider the effects your own book will have on your family, and how it will make them feel.

What are your spiritual or religious beliefs, and how have they shaped your life?

I believe that it is important to listen to our hearts when it comes to life choices. If something feels good and right within us and peace flows through as we think of and experience that thing, then that is the path to take for the time being. For us to hear and know what our heart feels, we first need to stop, be still, and empty our minds. You and I tend to make decisions based on intellect, but our minds are like sponges that absorb whatever they have been exposed to, so they are limited. We simply don't know what we don't know. It would take us multiple lifetimes to gain complete knowledge of the universe, so I think it is fair to say that our human understanding and intelligence is limited.

Faith is believing without seeing, having a *knowing within* without external evidence. Therefore, when it comes to other people's religions and spiritual practices, we have to be open to their faith without judgement. Let's be honest here – none of us knows the absolute truth, we simply listen to and follow our hearts to bring peace to our souls, and each of us has the right to do so. What I am saying is that it is important that we listen deep within ourselves and *feel* what is right for us without passing judgement on others for their personal beliefs.

I do not practice a particular faith, but I do believe in God, a divine, loving presence that is the source of my being. I have tread on different religious and spiritual paths, and I will continue to explore and experience many others. My feeling is that, ultimately, they all lead to the same, final destination, so the path we take is simply a matter of choice. No matter who we are, we all came from the same source, and we will all return to the same source through birth and death. In order for us to know the absolute truth of where we came from and where we are going, we will have to experience it for ourselves in death, so I think it is fair to say that none of us is in a hurry to know the truth right now. We are alive now, so let's make the most of life instead of worrying about death.

My father was brought up a Buddhist but converted to Catholicism when he married my mum. Even though we were raised as Catholics, I always had a curious mind and questioned everything. At times, I didn't "believe", but I was too scared not to, so I did as I was told. At around 12-years-old, I went in search of the truth and tried to read the Bible, but it made no sense to me. I could barely read a book without getting bored, never mind the Bible, but my longing for truth never left me.

I did eventually read it from cover to cover years later, which was challenging. Still, my questions remained unanswered, so now I go through life with an open heart, mind, and soul on an ever-evolving journey, seeking life's true and beautiful treasures.

WHAT DO WE NEED TO DO TO BECOME GOOD, KIND, AND LOVING HUMAN BEINGS?

We were born good, kind, and loving human beings, but some can forget who they are as they journey through life as they are conditioned by the world around them. Someone labelled as "bad" has simply lost his way, perhaps after having been subjected to a difficult upbringing without the love and guidance we might have had. Not everyone will agree with my way of thinking, but I choose to see people as souls, not physical beings. I choose to see others this way because I think that anger, resentment, and the lack of forgiveness poisons the world.

When we look into the eyes of a newborn child, there is only love and joy in them; nobody is *born* evil. It is essential we don't label each other as good or bad, as we all do what we believe is the best thing to do. I am in no way denying the many evil acts performed in the world, but we cannot look into someone else's heart and mind and know what is really going on deep within them. We don't know what physical and emotional scars they have attained in their lives that have driven them to do what they have done. Can any of us honestly say that if we had lived their lives, we would have turned out any differently? I choose not to judge others or their actions and hope that light will enter into their hearts again for them to see clearly.

Personally, I would love to see a world in which we are aware of each other's needs and are open about who we are with everyone we meet from a really young age, a world where we could simply say things such as "*I was hurt by what you said*," or "*Please, can you help me as I can't manage on my own*," but instead, we create stories in our minds and put up walls to divide ourselves from others in fear of being vulnerable or hurt in some way. Instead of asking for help, we keep quiet and struggle alone, putting up barriers to prevent others from seeing our vulnerabilities, essentially creating distance when what we really need and want is connection.

All conflict is due to a lack of understanding, communication, and of course, kindness. If we were more open and honest about what we really want and need from each other, then we would respond with more love and compassion. I believe our problems stem from not knowing our true selves, not loving our true selves, and not living openly as our true selves. If we were all happy and secure within ourselves and treated others with kindness, we would not be offended when others label us or feel compelled to label others.

If I were to call you a tree, would you be offended? No, because you know for sure that you are not a tree, but if I were to call you a pig, your mind might go on to make up stories about what I had meant, like "*She thinks I'm fat, ugly, and dirty*." Of course, if you know who you truly are and that nothing about you is pig-like, then my words would mean nothing.

By writing your life's story and your legacy you essentially take the time to get to know, love, and accept yourself, accept the imperfections and recognise that we are all works in progress, and become more forgiving, compassionate, and loving human beings. In essence, through improving ourselves, we improve the world.

IF YOU COULD DO ANY JOB RIGHT NOW WITH THE GUARANTEE OF 100% SUCCESS, REGARDLESS OF YOUR PRESENT SKILL SET, WHAT WOULD YOU DO AND WHY?

Why aren't we all simply living life, doing work that we love? Is it because we gave up on our dreams and gave into fear? Is it due to our lack of self-belief and worthiness? Is it because we are so comfortable in our day-to-day life and fear losing our sense of security? Have we told ourselves the opportunities are not within our reach, so we make do with what we have?

Whatever the reason, if we are not satisfied, something has to change, and that is either our attitudes – by renewing our energies and enthusiasm – or the situation itself. Let's not spend the rest of our working lives enduring monotony, wishing our lives away, waiting for retirement. Make a commitment to live each day doing a job you love, one that lights you up from the inside. Do not wait – make the changes now.

There is a powerful story about a man who finds an egg and places it in a chicken coop along with the other chicken eggs. What he does not know is that the egg belongs to an eagle that hatches and grows up with the other chicks. All of his life, the eagle does what the chickens do, eats what they eat, and flies only a few feet in the air just as they do. One day, the eagle looks up and is in awe of a beautiful creature gliding through the sky. He asks the other chickens, "What's that? I wish I could fly high in the clouds just like that."

They answer, "That's an eagle, and he's the king of the skies, but we can't fly that high because you and I are just chickens, and we belong down here, close to the ground."

The eagle lived his whole life longing to fly, wishing he was an eagle, but he sadly died, believing he was a chicken. He never came to know who he truly was, or that he was born to be a king of the skies.

We are here to open ourselves up to the truth of who we are to ourselves and our families. Let's dig deep to reveal the longings of our souls. We all have them. We all have dreams we bury due to fear, a lack of self-belief, or simply because it would take more effort than we are prepared to put into it, but to get something we have never had, we need to do something we have never done. We are here to discover the eagle in you, for you to take reign over your life and live the life you were born to live before it is too late.

Imagine you were *guaranteed* 100% success in life and could not fail – what would you do?

At the core, we all have the heart of an eagle and are the king or queen of our lives, so let's not follow the chickens or allow others to tell us who we are or that of which we are capable. Deep down, we know the longings of our souls, so let's listen to our beating hearts and try. We can choose to live a life safely cooped up, or we can spread our wings and truly fly.

WHAT AREAS OF YOUR LIFE ARE YOU THE HAPPIEST WITH, AND WHAT AREAS COULD YOU IMPROVE ON?

As we share our life's stories with our families, it is also important that they know what our daily lives are and what works well for us. They, too, will come to this time in their lives, God willing, and they will also want to know the challenges we faced on a daily basis, as well as what we did to improve our lives. I know that if I could speak to my parents right now, I would ask them the question above- which is why I am presenting it to you. I would also ask them what they struggle with the most in their everyday lives. It would be naïve of us to think that everyone's life runs smoothly at all times, in all areas, simultaneously. Our parents would certainly have had daily challenges just as we do, so it is important that we share how we deal with our daily challenges with our children. That is, if we want our children to overcome their challenges instead of accepting them as their fate.

As parents, we get on with managing our lives – kids, finances, food, emotions, everyone's wellbeing, relationships, work – but we can feel overwhelmed at times. We rarely take the time to reassess the quality of our lives or our happiness. Instead, we tend to look for distractions rather than solutions because it is simply easier. When we stop to acknowledge which areas need attention, however, and rearrange our priorities, ourselves, and our minds, our lives will flow with more ease. Distractions may give us the feeling of a temporary release from our daily challenges, such as a glass of wine or two in the evening, but instead of burying or numbing our feelings, it is essential that we make the necessary adjustments.

I am a big advocate of "self-care". Taking the time to tend to our physical, spiritual, and emotional needs first will calm those overwhelming moments and make us more loving, attentive, and present towards others. As parents, we are so used to putting our kids and everyone else before ourselves and our wellbeing that we have forgotten that we matter, too. We have to think about the kind of examples we are setting for our children. When we are not taking care of our wellbeing, or we are not able to show up as our best selves, it is usually those we love the most that see the worst version of ourselves. Therefore, it is essential to identify what needs attention in our lives and take the time to work on ourselves to be the happiest, healthiest people we can be for ourselves and our families.

Imagine your grown-up children at your current age and ask yourself, what kind of life do I desire for them? How do I want them to feel physically and emotionally? Do I want them to feel happier and healthier than I do right now? Do I want them to thrive in life or merely survive? Then, go and be the person you want your children to become, and do what needs to be done to make that happen. They do as we do, not as we say!

HAS YOUR LIFE TURNED OUT THE WAY YOU IMAGINED IT WOULD?

When we were young, full of wonder and enthusiasm for life, we imagined ourselves happily flowing through life with ease and grace. We never contemplated a life full of challenges, twists and turns, highs and lows, wins and losses. In time, we discovered that life does not always turn out as we expect it to. Everything we have experienced up to this point in time was meant to be and was meant to lead us here.

Now, as you write about your journey, you finally get to make sense of it all. You may have had a wonderful life and are here to share your joy, or you may have had a hard life and are here to share your nuggets of wisdom on how to survive. Either way, whatever you have to share will be valuable to your loved ones.

Life is shaped by the choices we make, and by sharing our experiences and emotions, and we may be able to help our families make better choices than we did. If we had personal struggles with alcohol or drug abuse, for example, and we talk openly about what was going on in our hearts and minds at the time, we may be able to help our families through that same struggle, avoiding the mistakes we made. None of us chooses to struggle, and we certainly do not aspire to be dependent on drugs and alcohol, but it happens.

So, even if you have had a hard life, the fact that you are able to open your heart through writing your legacy, means your personal struggles have served a purpose and will be a guiding light for future generations. I believe that any paths we take to lead us out of the darkness have to be shared. If we look back and see a wasted life instead of seeing a path to greater understanding, all of our pain and suffering was in vain. We can either live life regretting the past or learn from the challenges we face and use them to teach others a way out of theirs. Everything that you have gone through was all meant to be, to serve some greater purpose.

LOOKING BACK, WHAT WOULD YOU SAY YOUR GREATEST ACHIEVEMENTS HAVE BEEN?

One important aspect of recording a legacy and expressing gratitude for a life well-lived is acknowledging and celebrating the wins, big or small. Our small and perhaps insignificant wins in the eyes of the world can be our greatest wins, and that is on what we have to focus.

One of the greatest wins in my life was starting to run at the age of 45. Before then, I literally could not run a mile to save myself, or so I believed. I had never been able to run, even as a little girl. After being diagnosed with asthma in my late teens, my inability to run became imprinted in my mind. Though I only run three kilometres at a time, which is nothing for an experienced runner, for me, it is a great achievement. From not believing I could run to running three kilometres almost 30 years later, that was a big win for me. Since then, I have run more than 365 km a year, which equates to over 50 marathons, which is not too bad for a girl that could not run even a mile. I am not competing with anyone or trying to prove anything, but in my eyes, I am a winner.

For you, that win could be losing weight, repairing your marriage, overcoming substance abuse, overcoming depression, starting your own business, getting your health back on track, learning a new skill or language, climbing up the promotional ladder, buying your own home, being a good parent, learning to be a great cook, or writing your own book. Whatever your wins, embrace and celebrate them because you deserve to be valued by you.

All too often, we compare ourselves to others and think that we could have done better, and perhaps we could have; nevertheless, you and I have many personal wins that have made our lives worthwhile. The secret to contentment in life is not to have everything we want – it is progress.

As long as we are moving forward, no matter how slowly, the little steps are enough to remind us that we are getting somewhere. Some of us start to feel stuck as our children grow more independent. Our role as hands-on parents diminishes and perhaps we wonder: *What now?* However, we still have so much to give and receive in life, and there are many more wins ahead.

By answering these questions, focusing on the wins in your life, not only will you be reminded of all that you have achieved thus far, but it will open up your heart and mind to all of the passion and zest you still have within you. This journey that you are taking is yet another achievement that will make you and your family proud.

WHAT ARE YOUR BEST ATTRIBUTES, AND HOW HAVE EACH OF THEM SERVED YOU IN LIFE?

I do not know about you, but for me, talking about my attributes is one of the hardest things to do; however, it is an essential part of the work you are doing here. I designed this book as a journey through life, not only as a legacy for our children but to look deeper within ourselves to see the wonder and greatness each of us has. Most of us can easily list all of our shortcomings and insecurities as they tend to flow easily into our thoughts and out of our mouths, but we have to look a little deeper for our attributes as we can be guilty of hiding them away.

I can only speak from personal experience, but I rarely come across people who are sure of themselves. We are all too quick to say negative things about ourselves as if it is okay to do so, but how often do we talk about ourselves positively? Do we want our children to become adults who focus on their positive attributes or the negative ones as they journey through life? I am not talking about narcissism, which is, in essence, bumping yourself up, thinking you are above others. I am talking about seeing yourself as if you are your own best friend and picking out your best qualities as a human being.

Imagine living with someone who constantly complains about you and puts you down every chance they have, criticising your every move, telling you that you are not good enough, not attractive enough, and not smart enough. How would that make you feel? Would you tolerate the abuse? I did. I lived with such a person for over 40 years before I decided to make friends with her and find out what was really going on beneath the surface. Once I got to know who she really was deep down, I realised that she was a hurt little girl in desperate need of some love and acceptance. I began to listen to her, support her, nurture her, and love her, and she blossomed into a powerful force of love. She had been in pain, and I had shut her out, but all she needed was love and reassurance that she was worthy of love. When I made peace with her, I saw the greatness within her. She has since become my strength, my fuel, and my very best friend. She is me.

It took me many years to accept myself because I had not done the work of knowing and loving myself. I have an open and honest heart, I care deeply about all people, and I believe I am a kind and loving soul. I am also determined, and I do exactly what I set out to do, which I like in myself. It is not easy to write about what we like about ourselves, but by putting it down in black and white, we begin to own our truths. It is essential that we find our inner-shines, to love and accept who we are.

As you dig deep, remember to think of yourself as being your own best friend. We all have good and not so good attributes, but focus on what you *do* like about yourself. If your children were exactly like you, would you be proud of them, or would you play down their best attributes?

WHAT GOOD QUALITIES AND ATTRIBUTES DO YOU LIKE TO SEE IN OTHERS?

As human beings, we subconsciously judge each other by our own standards. We expect others to be as we want them to be, but who said our way is the best way? Are we so perfect that everyone else should live up to our standards? We are doing the work in this book to open ourselves up, to know the truth of who we are and the way we think. The truth can hurt at times- especially when we begin to accept responsibility for our own mistakes, causing us to feel some level of pain and regret but when we know they are growing pains, it makes the pain easier to bear. I, too, went through growing pains, having taken this journey before you, and I had to take a good look at myself to face my demons, but it was all worth it. Now, I see life with more clarity, and I am so much happier for it.

Being aware of our thoughts, words, and behaviours enable us to recognise judgement within us towards others, which allows us to end it. None of us is perfect, after all, so how dare we judge others?

Personally, I like to see people being kind, loving, compassionate, and open with each other. I do my best to be that kind of person, too, because these are the standards I set for myself. However, I know they may not be everyone's standard. We all have personal core values, and when we meet new people with whom we "just click", it is because a lot of our core values are in alignment. It is what we have in common with others that attracts us to them and binds us together.

When I began opening up to others to reveal my true self, I came to realise that we are a lot more alike than we are different. No matter who we are, what our backgrounds may be, where we come from, or how different we all are, when we look *deep* enough, we are able to see and feel the soul of another, to feel that deep connection and oneness within us. We are all made up of the same energy, essence, and matter. What separates us are our thoughts and ideas about who we think others *should* be, and the labels we use to define ourselves. Once we shed our labels and focus on seeing the good qualities in ourselves and each other, we create deeper connections and love in our lives. At the core, we are essentially still the bundles of love and joy that were born into the world, and when we see it in ourselves, we cannot deny it in others.

Question 70

THINK ABOUT YOUR PHYSICAL APPEARANCE. IMAGINE YOU HAD AN IDENTICAL TWIN WHO YOU LOVED DEARLY AND DESCRIBE HIM/HER.

Although we all know that one cannot judge a book by its cover and that it is what we are on the inside that matters, there is no denying that you and I and everyone else fixates on looks. I have never actually met anyone that gives no thought whatsoever to her outward appearance, which is why I have included such a question in this book. We rarely talk about our appearances, and we try not to make it an issue, but it is never very far from our thoughts. Even when we are happy with who we are on the inside, our outward appearance tends to hijack our self-worth, unless, of course, we are in the midst of a life trauma or illness. If we were to really think about it, we would realise how baffling it is that we obsess over our appearances when, deep down, we know it has no bearing whatsoever on our value. Still, it is a constant struggle to let this go. It does not seem to matter how "perfect" someone may look to others – underlying issues of self-worth often linger deep within a person. If I said that I did not care about what I looked like, I would be lying, but I *do* tend to focus more on my health rather than my looks.

As parents, most of us do our best to shape and teach our children to become resilient and confident adults. Due to our unresolved issues, however, we inadvertently pass our own shortcomings and insecurities on to our offspring by the way we look and the way we talk about ourselves in their presence. As I mentioned earlier, my mum passed on her insecurities about her appearance to me. Because I am now aware of this, I am careful about how I speak about myself around my children. It is only when we recognise our negative self-talk that we are able to break old patterns and be more conscious of the words we use to describe ourselves.

Can you remember when your baby was in your arms, looking up at you with pure love in his or her eyes and adoration glowing from his/her tiny face? You could not have been more perfect to your children then, and they felt the love in your heart. They were not focused on whether you had clear skin, good bone structure, or straight teeth. You could have had boils and missing teeth, and they would have loved you exactly how you were, so our insecurities do not lie with what we look like to those who love us. This is about how we feel about ourselves in comparison to others.

With this question, I ask you to imagine that you had an identical twin because in doing so, I believe you will all be a little kinder to yourself. If I asked you what you did not like about your outward appearance, I am sure you could answer really quickly without too much thought, but because I am asking you to focus on your physical attributes, it will take a little more effort. As you do this, imagine your children doing the same thing. Would you encourage them to see their good attributes or focus on their not so good ones? This may sound cliché, but beauty does truly shine out through the soul and has nothing to do with the shape and form of our features and bodies, so do not judge your own book by the cover either. Simply enjoy the beauty of your life's story.

How did you deal with heartbreak?

There are many levels of heartbreak and varying degrees of pain. Losing loved ones to death is one kind of heartbreak; having someone reject you and your love is quite another – this is what we are going to talk about here. When people we love die we are left broken-hearted, but we come to terms with it in time as we have no other choice. When someone *chooses* not to be with us, however, or someone chooses someone else over us, we tend to take it personally. If we do not deal with the pain of rejection, we essentially carry the baggage of the past with us through life, compromising all future relationships.

When our hearts are broken, the pain can be unbearable. We wonder if we will ever be happy again, as we cannot imagine life without that person. Our egos also take a good old beating as we begin to doubt our self-worth, our lovability, and who we are as human beings. We ask ourselves poor quality questions, such as *What's wrong with me? Why don't they love me? Am I not good enough?* We seek answers but always come up blank. We do not consider that perhaps they, too, were in pain and left us because they just were not happy. After all, if we loved them unconditionally, wouldn't their happiness be important to us, without conditions? Would we want someone to stay with us out of a sense of duty, or do we want them to stay because they love us completely and want to be with us?

Blessings can come from every circumstance, and if we look closely enough, we will find them. Through being broken open, we are given the opportunities to look inside ourselves to see what we are made of. In time, as we put ourselves back together, we realise that we have learned valuable life lessons that have helped us navigate through life, leading us to brighter and better paths, giving us the ability to look deeper within ourselves and tap into our inner strength and the beauty of our souls.

Whether we still carry the pain of our once broken hearts that we have never truly moved on from, or whether we are here as shoulders for our children to cry on, broken hearts need to be addressed. These feelings cannot just be brushed under the carpet, never to be spoken of again. They need to be honoured and fully accepted, or they become a weight too heavy to carry, and they can affect the whole trajectory of our lives. We cannot change the past, and we cannot make people love us, but we can learn to love ourselves, to forgive those who have hurt us, and learn to let go. Our children *will* have their hearts broken, and they will experience struggles in life, so we need to share our stories with them, so they know that they, too, will come out on the other side, better and stronger because of them.

WHAT DOES A LOVING RELATIONSHIP LOOK AND FEEL LIKE TO YOU?

Love can mean so many things to different people, and there are many variations of love. If someone were to say, "I love chicken," for example, would that mean they really love chicken or love to eat chicken? This shows two completely different meanings of love using exactly the same words. So, before we can talk about love in our own stories, we have to define our personal ideas of what love looks and feels like to us. For me, love is the foundation of life and the core of all successful relationships, whether in our relationship with others, ourselves, nature, faith, work, or the world in general. When we have love in all areas of life, we feel content and happy. However, when our personal relationships do not work well, it can affect all other areas of our lives if we do not have sufficient love for ourselves first, resulting in our lives falling apart.

One key lesson that I have learnt in my life is that we do not *need* another person to make us whole. We may spend our lives looking for someone to be our "*other* half", to make us feel complete, but we are not half-beings.

The emptiness we feel is not from the lack of a person with whom to spend our lives but a lack of love for ourselves. It is the longing to connect with the deepest parts of our soul. The only place we need to look for that other-half is within, learning to know ourselves, love ourselves, and be ourselves. Once we do, we will make better choices. We become whole beings, seeking out life partners, not to fill the emptiness within our hearts, but for someone to grow and evolve alongside us.

My definition of a loving relationship is a deep bond between two people that goes beyond the physical; it is the connection of two souls. True intimacy runs far deeper than merely two bodies coming together. It is the bond between two souls that is intertwined with love, one that frees us to bare and share our true selves, our fears, our joys, and our deepest desires with each other, and at the same time, support one another through life's ups and downs without judgement and without the need to control.

We all have individual needs and desires that only we can express. Some of us crave physical intimacy and need to be touched and held to feel loved, some crave time spent in deep conversation or to be told they are loved, and some need to be shown through loving acts of kindness or thoughtful gifts. If we do not bare our souls and truly express what we need from each other, our relationships can become strained, so in loving relationships, communication is key.

Some believe that being a part of a loving relationship means that we belong to each other, but people are not possessions. No one can own us. If we truly love one another, we would not try to control each other or dictate what the other can or cannot do with his life. It is about a partnership of togetherness, desiring the very best for each other, mind, body, and spirit.

Neither our life partners nor our children belong to us, nor are they a part of us; they are whole, complete beings on their own, just as we all are. We are simply a source of love and support for them. If we squeeze them too tightly, hoping to keep them close, we risk them slipping through our fingers.

We all crave love and loving relationships, but it is paramount for us to remember that other people cannot love us to make us happy. It is not their responsibility to fill our hearts with love – it is ours. By opening up about what loving relationships mean to us, we allow our loved ones to see into our hearts, to understand what inspires and motivates us to love the way we do.

WHAT AREAS OF YOUR LIFE ARE YOU MOST HAPPY WITH AND WHY?

We all experience good times and bad. When we focus on what is working well, we feel happier and more in control of our destinies. However, it is important that we do not forget to simply stop to assess our lives, carry out a life audit, and take inventory of our feelings. Once we do, we will see what needs work and what is working well. What areas of your life work well – your health and wellbeing, career, relationships, friendships, finances, family? We can get so caught up in our day to day lives at times that we neglect to notice the important areas of our lives that need attention.

When I first began practising gratitude daily, my eyes were opened to all of the good and beauty by which I was surrounded. I was not happy within myself at the time, but I decided to trust what I had learnt and put it into practice, and it worked. I began to see that my life was not as grim as I had told myself it was. I spent time working on seeing what worked well in my life instead of what was not. The more I opened up, the more beauty I saw in my outer world, where I lived, the sun, the clouds, the fields, the buildings, the sea, and all the beautiful things in nature. I also became more aware of what was not working, but instead of complaining about it, I took steps towards gaining knowledge about what I needed to *do* to make my life better. Gratitude seemed a little too simplistic, but looking at my life differently made my life look better. I had been so focused on the problems that I failed to look for the solutions. Once I began to see small, positive changes happening within myself, my heart and mind were opened to greater possibilities, and I was hooked.

We can all feel stuck in life at times, and the road ahead can look dim, but it is only our perspectives that are clouded. Because our minds are clouded with doubt and negativity, we can only see the fog ahead, so we first have to clear our minds. Clear out all the unnecessary junk clouding our judgement and vision to enable us to see clearly again; essentially clearing a pathway out.

The work that we are doing here, answering these questions and writing your story, tidies up your mind, giving you a clearer perspective

A happy and purposeful life is available for every one of us, no matter the age or stage we are at in our life journeys. If we choose to have faith, find solutions, and take the necessary steps forward, focusing on gratitude, then a clearer vision and renewed enthusiasm for life is inevitable.

ON WHAT AREAS OF YOUR LIFE DO YOU NEED TO WORK? WHAT ADVICE OR WISDOM CAN YOU SHARE WITH YOUR LOVED ONES CONCERNING THESE AREAS?

As parents of growing children, we already know they do not always like to take advice from us. In fact, if they are teens, they may even do the exact opposite of what we suggest. Nevertheless, they will benefit greatly from learning about our experiences in the past and present, how we got ourselves into certain challenging situations, and also how we dealt with them. Some of our challenges may be resolved, and some may be ongoing, but all of our experiences will serve our offspring in some way. If not now, perhaps they will in the future.

None of us is perfect, neither parent nor child, and we all make mistakes. Our children may even be wiser than us as wisdom does not always come hand in hand with age, especially if we do not learn from our mistakes.

Let's take our health, for example. We all know what we *should* be eating and drinking. We also know that we have to get sufficient exercise, rest, and fresh air, but do we follow through? I am vigilant about my health because of my brush with death, so I naturally passed on what I learned to my children. I have shared my wisdom, and now I simply have to hope that they learn from my mistakes and pay more attention to their health than I did at their age. We all want the best for our kids. We want them to live happy, healthy, joy-filled lives full of love, but we cannot make this happen – our children have to want it and create it for themselves. We can share our wisdom, but the rest is up to them.

Depending on what our current priorities are, all of us have areas in need of a little more attention than we have been giving them of late. We have sacrificed our time and energy to serve our greater purpose at times, but it is vitally important that we get our priorities into the right order first. Many years ago, I met a lovely family with five beautiful kids between the ages of 12 years and six months. When I walked into their home, it was a shambles. There were clothes and toys everywhere, and I could feel myself tensing up in all the mess and confusion. The children, though, were so happy, friendly, kind-hearted, and polite, and it was a delight to be in their company. As I chatted with the mother, she simply looked around her home and said, "Either I can dedicate my time to keeping my house clean and tidy, or I can spend my time cooking healthy meals for my family and giving each of them one on one time with me. I choose my family." Those few words left a deep and lasting impression on me, and I knew then what kind of mother I wanted to become.

This question will help you to step back to see the bigger picture in your life and help you to re-evaluate your priorities. You will be reminded of what is important and what needs your attention most at this time. Sometimes, we get caught up in mindless activities, wasting our time and energy on things that mean nothing to us, so being here answering these questions will not only get us back on track - it will wake us up.

WHAT IS ONE THING IN YOUR LIFE THAT REMINDS YOU THAT LIFE IS TRULY BEAUTIFUL?

The happiest people I have come across in my life are those that have fallen and fallen hard. In a way, they had to be knocked out to come to their senses. Regardless of their circumstances, whether they were depressed and suicidal, or had lost a loved one, it took them hitting rock bottom to see things clearly.

I am ashamed to say that I never believed that depression was a real condition until it hit me. I had always been so determined to succeed, but when I found myself on the metaphorical ground unable to pick myself up, I couldn't believe it. How could this have happened to *me*, the go-getter? Well, it did, but I chose to believe it had happened "for me" and not "to me". This was my wakeup call, the door to my life's purpose, which led me to know and love myself. It also led me to the beginning of a new and better life.

Some people spend their lives waiting out their time, and some grab hold of life with both hands and squeeze every last drop of it out, making the most of every single day. Ultimately, how we live our lives is simply down to choice. We do not have to hit rock bottom or wait for life to knock us down to appreciate life. We can decide to start living today and with more joy, but *we* have to make it happen. How? By changing our minds and opening our eyes and hearts to all of the beauty in and around us.

The secret to seeing the beauty in life is to look for it, to open our awareness to *everything* around us. *Stop* for a moment and watch a spider spinning its web, the birds flying in the sky above us, the clouds gliding and transforming into shapes, the sun setting or rising, or simply looking into the eyes of an innocent, happy baby to see the beauty and wonder within them. It is truly fascinating when we actually stop and pay close attention. It calms our hearts and minds and brings peace to our inner-world, giving us the strength to face the outer world with more enthusiasm. This may sound a bit *new-age*, but by becoming consciously aware of our surroundings and more mindful in all we do, we are reminded of the true beauty of life. Do not just take my word for it – I challenge you to try it for yourself.

Sometimes, we need to remind ourselves and others about the true treasures in life. These treasures are not fame, fortune, fancy cars, exotic holidays, and the like that make life beautiful; they are those small moments of pure joy when time stands still. I see and feel these moments when I am out in nature,when I am cuddled up with my kids, when I am swimming in the sea or meditating in my garden. This may be far from your idea of bliss – yours might be fishing or sailing – but whatever it is, take time to enjoy this life and revel in its beauty.

WHAT ARE YOU MOST GRATEFUL FOR IN YOUR LIFE?

When we think of all the things for which we are grateful, we should not limit ourselves to the happy moments. Our troubles and challenges can turn out to be our greatest blessings, but that can only happen if we decide to learn from them instead of complaining about them. We do not get to choose which cards we are dealt, but we can choose how we play them, and how we react towards them. We can let them drag us down, or we can learn something new about ourselves that will bring brighter perspectives.

As a parent, the first thing most of us will say is that we are grateful for our children, yet being a parent is challenging. If we could take away the challenge of parenting, would we? Absolutely not, because we are committed parents who love our children. No matter how much we struggle with the many aspects of raising a family, we are and always will be truly grateful for our children. Even when they are fully grown with families of their own, they will always be the centres of our worlds. So, gratitude is not about being grateful for everything that is working well – it is about appreciating all facets of life and the whole life experience. We may not love our work, for example, but we can still be grateful, even if we find it challenging because it allows us to earn money to pay bills and live comfortably. We can be grateful for our partners and spouses, even if we find them difficult at times as they also support us emotionally, financially, and physically on our journeys through life. We do not have to be happy to be grateful, but we do have to be grateful to be happy.

I have practised gratitude every day for a few years now. The first thing every morning and the last thing at night, I write down at least three things for which I am grateful to remind me of all the blessings my life has to offer. It starts my day off on a positive note, and I fall asleep with a peaceful heart at night. Personally, I am grateful for all of my life experiences, good and bad. Each of my experiences has enriched my life in its own way. Some were a slap in the face to wake me up while others reminded me of how wonderful life can be. They taught me that I am fully responsible for the state of my mind, health, emotions, and happiness. I am grateful for the life I have been given, and I will not waste any of it. Gratitude has taught me that whatever comes into my life comes *for me* to help me to grow and evolve, to awaken me to the true treasures of life.

WHO ARE YOU MOST GRATEFUL FOR AND WHY?

Life is wonderful because of the love and deep connections we have with each other. Without people in our lives, life would feel empty and meaningless, but to have loving relationships, we have to consciously create, nurture, and build connections with others, as it rarely happens automatically.

I recall having a conversation with an elderly lady I knew years ago. Every time we spoke, she would mention how lonely she was, but because I didn't live nearby, I could do nothing to help.

She lived in an apartment building alongside many other people of her age, but despite living so close to these people for over 40 years, she had not developed any deep friendships. On this particular occasion, after hearing her complain about being on her own, I suggested that she knock on the door of one of her neighbours and perhaps invite them over for a cuppa and chat, but she was appalled at my suggestion and told me so.

"It's not my place to invite them. They should come and ask me!" she said.

She simply could not see the irony of what she was saying. I tried to explain to her that if every lonely person thought the way she did, nothing would ever change, but I could not get through to her. Sure enough, nothing changed, and sadly, this poor lady died lonely because she was unwilling to change or do anything to improve her situation. She was just too proud to ask for some company and build deeper connections.

Whatever we want to have more of in life, be it joy, wealth, great health, or wonderful relationships, we have to create them for ourselves. We all have access to all the treasures in life, but it all depends on how much time, effort, and attention we pay to significant areas, including people with whom we want to share our lives.

This question is to remind you of all the wonderful people you have in your life. We are often so distracted with what is going on in the world that we neglect to see what is right in front of us. When it comes to those we love, we spend time running about, serving our clients, co-workers, bosses, and customers, giving them the best parts of us, but when we get home at the end of the day, our families get the dregs and nasty sediment that remains.

I am not only grateful for my family, my beautiful sisters, and my friends, but I am also grateful for all of the wise teachers who have greatly enriched my life. Even though my parents are no longer alive, I am truly grateful for them and all the sacrifices they made. I owe it to them and myself to be happy. I honour them with gratitude for the gift of my life.

WHO HAS BEEN AN INSPIRATION IN YOUR LIFE, AND WHY?

We are all influenced by the people we are surrounded by, just as we also influence others, whether we want to or not. Our actions, attitudes, words, and behaviours impact the world in some way, so it is important that we decide whether we want to be inspirations in the lives of others.

Regardless of how unkind life has been to us, our reactions to our circumstances are what counts. We cannot change what happens, but we can change our attitudes and behaviours in the face of challenges.

I think it is fair to say that those who have inspired us the most did not do so because they lived perfect lives, but because of the strength they displayed in the face of challenges. I imagine that they were not the kind of people who ran away from their difficulties, but instead, fought to overcome them. With this in mind, we can move forwards with a clearer understanding of the kind of examples we want to be, to simply decide whether we want to be inspirations to others through being sources of love and strength.

If you are currently in need of some inspiration, be mindful of who you spend time with, what you watch and listen to, and the kind of books you read. The quality of our company and surroundings determines who inspires us and in turn, how we inspire others. Hanging out with negative people will not yield positivity in our lives. I am by no means saying that we have to cut all ties with negative people, but instead of being infected by their negative mindset, we can become sources of inspiration in their lives. We may need to put a little distance between these people and us for a time until we get our mindsets back on track, but ultimately, by helping ourselves, we help others, too.

Just as we need to seek out friends and nurture our relationships with others, we need to seek out people who inspire us, and who we look at in awe as we can see their inner-shine. They do not have to be grand personalities but people who touch our hearts and souls, those who ignite the spark of hope and wonder within us. I have had too many sources of inspiration in my life to mention, but I put that down to my unrelenting search for knowledge, wisdom, and inspiration in all things and all people, but if I were to name one, it would be the Dalai Lama. His ability to see the love in all things, people, and situations inspires me beyond measure, and I aspire to become like him.

IF YOU COULD GO BACK TO VISIT YOUR YOUNGER SELF, WHAT KEY PIECES OF ADVICE WOULD YOU GIVE YOURSELF?

If I had been asked this question six or seven years ago, I could have easily written a long list of all the things I would have told myself to avoid, including all of the people and situations who had crossed my path. Today, however, I can honestly say, hand on heart, that I would not change a single thing about my past because I would not be the person sitting here right now if it were not for all that has happened. I sometimes have to pinch myself when I realise how far I have come, from a time when I felt powerless, wishing I could fast-forward my life to the end, to wondering whether I will have enough time to write all of the books I want to write.

Because of my transformation, I know I am absolutely qualified to teach what I have learned with the hope of helping others to do the same. I teach that life does not change by itself; you have to actively bring about change. You need to search your soul and love and forgive yourself as well as others. This does not happen overnight, but progress comes about by taking consistent steps forward every day, allowing your life to unfold, creating a path of happiness and fulfilment as you grow.

Speaking to my younger self, I would simply say, "Be true to yourself and listen to your heart. You can be and do whatever your heart desires because you have all that you need deep within you. Trust the whisperings of your soul and don't ever let anyone tell you who you are. Take the time to know yourself, love yourself and always show up as your true and authentic self. Don't dim your light or hide in the shadows because you are more than enough."

As you contemplate the advice you would *give* your younger self, think about what you wish you would have known about then. I wish I had been taught the importance of creating a deep inner connection with my true self, but would I have been ready to listen? Would any of us have listened to the advice we were given? Would we even understand what we were talking about without the experience of life behind us? Every challenge, every joy, and every experience has brought us here, right now, and we simply have to trust that it was all meant to be somehow, and accept that this was the right path for us. Regardless of what sage advice we receive, some things can only be learned the hard way.

What are some of the nicest things people have said about you that made you smile? For what do people regularly compliment you?

Without a doubt, it is so much easier to give compliments than it is to receive them. I was always so uncomfortable when I was given one. I did not know what to say, so I either said nothing or deflected by saying, "Really?" Saying thank you felt as if I were being boastful, as if I were saying, "Yeah, I know," but once I realised that it was unkind not to accept the gift of a compliment, I made a conscious effort to change my ways. I have now learned to simply say, "Thank you, you're so kind!" A compliment is indeed a gift, and when we treat it like one, it can brighten the day of the giver and receiver and even leave a deep impression on them. Think of the impact of a compliment – this quote accurately describes it: "When you see something beautiful in someone, tell them. It may take seconds to say, but for them, it could last a lifetime."

I am the kind of person who will go up to complete strangers to tell them how beautiful they look or how kindly they have behaved – it is just who I am. It makes people feel valued for their good qualities and inspires them to keep going. We know how wonderful it feels to hear words of kindness and gratitude, so it is important that we treat others in the same way. It is not about feeding their egos – it is about showing appreciation, spreading good and kind energy, and reminding others they are valued and significant in this world.

I remember something an ex-boyfriend from when I was 15 once told me. He came up to me out of the blue one evening while I was out with my friends and said, "You were the best thing that ever happened in my life," and promptly walked away, without waiting for a response. This was 15 years *later*. I was gob-smacked! He was not the love of my life then, and he had not broken my heart, but I do remember being upset with him at the time because he had one of his friends dump me instead of facing me himself. His comment all those years later was one of the most memorable moments of my life. He clearly did not expect anything back from me, but he just wanted to let me know that I had meant something to him, and it was lovely to hear that I had made a lasting impression on him. Sadly, he died in a car crash a few years ago, which makes that moment even more precious to me. Instead of him being my first proper boyfriend who dumped me, he became the man whose words will stay with me forever.

We have no idea the impact our words have on others, whether complimentary or critical, so we have to be conscious of the words we use and the way we speak to others, but when our intentions are pure, and our words are said with love, we cannot go wrong.

IF YOU WERE GRANTED A WISH TO SPEND AN ENTIRE DAY WITH ANYONE, WHO WOULD THAT BE AND WHY?

One part of me would love to spend an entire day with any of the world's greatest spiritual leaders, such as Lao Tzu, Gandhi, Buddha, or Jesus. I would love to learn from them and understand who they were. The truth, however, is that if I were granted such a wish, I would want to spend an entire day with my late mother. I only had her for 35 years of my life, and more than half of them were spent fighting with her, so I never had the chance to really know who she was on a soul-level. In fact, if I had an entire day with her, I would ask her these 101 questions because I still have so many unanswered questions about her. That being said, the fact that I still have so many unanswered questions has been the driving force and reason for creating and writing this book.

You are making a valuable piece of history here. Even if you only write a few lines and answer a few of the questions, every insight into your heart and mind is of great value. When our parents are alive, we simply cannot imagine the sense of loss and emptiness we feel when they pass. Before my parents passed, I avoided thinking about when the time would come because the thought alone was painful enough. Death is a natural part of life, however, and something of which we have to be fully aware to remind us that our time together is limited.

I originally created this book as a step-by-step programme using these questions. When it was complete, I asked my sister if she thought it was something she would like to do for her teenage son, Joey, but she said that she talks to him all the time, and he knows everything he needs to know about her life. I would be lying if I said I was not disappointed, and we did have a bit of a heated discussion on this subject, as sisters do. In the end, I accepted her views and realised that everyone will not be as passionate about the value of this work as I am, but I did end the discussion with, "Ask Joey what his thoughts are?"

The next day, my sister came with her tail between her legs, saying that Joey would love nothing more than to have her write a legacy for him. *Result*: she began writing, and even though she does not dedicate much time to this work, what she has already done will be of tremendous value to Joey one day. Even though our children will not be able to talk to us in the inevitable future, our thoughts and words will be there to comfort them when they need us the most.

WHAT PERSONAL LIFE CHALLENGES REMINDED YOU OF HOW STRONG YOU REALLY ARE?

The one thing human beings have in common, regardless of how rich our lives are, is that each and every one of us has experienced personal challenges, lost loved ones, and faced personal demons. One of my close friends and a former client used to jokingly say that it never seems to rain on me or Nicola (my former business partner) because from the outside, we had it all: looks, success, friendship, a great business, and we were always laughing and joking. The reality was that we each had our personal challenges and some deep, dark insecurities that were hidden from the world.

We are all guilty of looking at other people and making up stories about the kind of people they are, what they are thinking, and how they are feeling. The truth is that we don't have a clue what is going on inside the hearts and minds of anyone else, even the people closest to us.

When I was in the depths of my depression, I still had a smile on my face. I put on an act, but inside, I was dying. It was so hard to hold in all of that pain. I lost a lot of weight, and people would say how great I looked.

Looking back at old photos from that period, I did look the picture of health and happiness, and none of the pain going on within me could be seen on the surface. Despite eating plenty and desperately trying to gain a few pounds, the weight continued to fall off of me. If I had been well at the time, I would have been delighted with my weight loss, but I was concerned for my wellbeing, which is ironic, considering that I really wanted to vanish from the earth. I also had my children to take care of, and they were my main concern. Even though I wished my life would fast forward to the end, taking my own life was never an option for me. I had seen and felt the effects of suicide many times after losing friends and family members, and I knew the devastation it would leave behind, so that was out of the question.

So, there I was in the darkest period of my life, the picture of health in the eyes of others, in great shape, and with a smile on my face, yet nobody could see my pain and suffering. Looking back, that suffering was one of the greatest blessings in my life. Why? Because I learnt so much about myself and about life. I learnt empathy and compassion as my eyes really opened to the world around me. I no longer saw people in the same way, and no longer made judgements about people's actions or behaviours because I realised that we just do not know how others feel. We do not know the depths of their emotional or physical suffering. The experience truly humbled me.

When I broke through, I also realised my strength, and that the love I had for my children was far greater than any obstacle that could ever get in the way of me being the best mother I could be. Essentially, my love for them saved me.

When answering this question, consider the life lessons you learned from experiencing personal struggles and how you can pass on those important lessons to your children.

WHAT KIND OF PERSON ARE YOU?

It is said that people are either drains or radiators in life; we either radiate energy and love or we drain it from those surrounding us. However, we can choose which one we want to be.

Depending on where we are in our lives, the answer to this question may vary, but if we discover that we are "drains" when we want to be "radiators", we can change right now. All it takes is the decision to change.

I am really short-sighted and have needed glasses since I was a little girl, but I hated them, so I never wore them, and I spent the first 17 years of my life essentially blind. I could not see people waving at me. Whilst they thought I was ignoring them, I had no idea of their presence, so I did not feel guilty. I only realised what had happened after they told me.

My point is that we do not know what we do not know, so we cannot feel bad for things that happen when we are unaware of our behaviours. However, when we do become aware, being open and honest and examining those behaviours is imperative.

I am now a radiator, and I have made a personal promise to myself to stay on this path. Looking back, however, during my darkest time, I was most certainly a drain. I felt powerless over my life, and even though I hid it from the outside world, I was a drain on my family. Until I was able to see myself clearly, I was unable to make the decision to change. Once I saw my hand in life, I could take the necessary steps forward to become a radiator of love and light again. *I* had to change.

Through answering this question, you may discover that you are the negative person who constantly complains and drains the energy from those around you. If that does not please you, there is no need to feel bad – you simply did not know what you did not know. When we take full responsibility for our lives and behaviours and make the necessary changes instead of blaming and complaining, a pathway forward will begin to unfold, and we can take back control of our lives and happiness.

How do you feel when you are around joyful people?

My understanding of the difference between living joyfully and being happy is that joy is a state of inner-wellbeing that is not controlled by external factors, while happiness is a temporary feeling of elevation depending on external circumstances. Another way to think of it is that joy comes from the soul, and happiness comes from the mind and emotions. My current journey is one of joy. I am still a work in progress, but the deeper I go into learning about myself and mastering my inner-world, the less I am affected by the external world.

Sometimes, I can be out for a walk in nature, and I am filled with a sense of pure love, inner-peace, and joy as I watch the sunset, observe the form of the clouds, watch the birds fly above me in the sky, and see the beauty in a simple flower. At times, even tears of joy run down my face from an intense feeling of love and gratitude for life. Feeling joy goes beyond the thrill that comes from the excitement of physical activity or an event – it is a quiet sense of oneness with everything.

Sitting here, writing brings me a great sense of joy as the flow of love from my soul pours freely into my work. Because I know how wonderful it feels, it is my wish that every human being can experience the feeling of joy for herself. It is already within us as we were born into this world as bundles of joy, and we simply need to search deep within ourselves to release it.

Although this is my idea of joy, you will have your own thoughts and feelings about what joy looks and feels like to you. I am not here to tell you what to think or what to feel. I use my own experiences only to encourage and inspire you to express your thoughts and emotions openly.

As well as talking about how you feel when around joyful people, consider what joy means to you. Write about what brings you joy and describe how it feels to you. Your legacy is not about producing quality writing to make your stories look nice or to paint a pretty picture – it is about leaving them a little piece of who *you* truly are. After all, you are an original!

WHAT AND WHO MAKES YOU SMILE?

The hard but simple truth is that most of the people in our lives are actually reflections of who we are, which means that if we are surrounded by miserable faces, we must look in the mirror to check the expression on our own faces. Again, this is about becoming aware of how we show up in life and the energy we emit. There is no denying that there are some beautiful souls that simply light up a room with their smiles. Whenever we are in their presence, we cannot help but smile ourselves. I aspire to be one of those people. Call me crazy, but I love nothing more than to see people smile and live their lives with love and joy.

One thing I always say is that "We can't make people happy, but we can make them smile." Human beings are social beings, and we were born to live our lives together, interacting with one another. Sometimes, all people need is to be seen and heard to feel included, which alone is enough to make them smile.

In the town I grew up in Scotland, a "Waste Operative", named George, has always had the special gift for making people smile. For as long as I can remember, he has kept our streets clean and tidy, brightening our local "High

Street" with his presence. It is always a joy to see him because he always has something funny to say. Mind you, it is not always what he says or how good or how bad his jokes are – it is more about the energy he radiates. He is a ray of sunshine on an often dreary day in our small Scottish town, and he plays a role in the life of our town that is about more than just making it clean and beautiful. He injects joy into the community and makes a difference in people's lives, simply by being himself. My point is that it does not matter who we are or what we do for a living – we can all make a difference in the lives of others. You and I can also be a George, simply by opening our eyes to the people around us and our behaviours and actions. The next level is being aware of how we interact with the world and how people respond to us.

When we spend time with people, do they leave with a smile or a frown? Do we include them in our lives or exclude them? Are we showing up as the best versions of ourselves, or is there bitterness within us, spilling out and hurting others?

If we want to be surrounded by smiles, then we must spread them. Like George, we can *all* be a light and make this world brighter, one person and one smile at a time.

WHAT ACTS OF LOVE AND KINDNESS HAVE YOU SHOWERED ON OTHERS IN YOUR LIFE THAT MADE THEM SMILE?

We all have the ability to put smiles on faces. The more smiles we spread, the brighter and lighter we feel and the happier we become. In my next book, which is already written, I have a chapter titled "Selfish Service" because when we are in the service of others, doing what we can to lift them up makes us feel amazing. So, I think it is fair to say that helping others is also about making ourselves feel good.

We are innately wired to care for other human beings; we came into the world that way. Just look at how babies and toddlers react towards each other – they do not judge their peers by their race, creed, gender, or social status, and they are naturally loving and caring. Though we may not always show that side of us, the deep-seated care and compassion remain within us. Some people may have forgotten their true natures, but we are all love at our cores, even if we cannot always see it in others.

If you did not know this already, there is great power in a smile. We do not have to be happy to smile, but when we smile, we feel so much happier. Just as the brain can command your finger to touch your nose, it can command your lips to smile. Let's do a little experiment: wherever you are right now, put the biggest, cheesiest smile you can muster on your face and hold it for five seconds. Now, notice how you feel and the look on your face. I will bet you are still smiling or feeling brighter. If you do not feel the difference, check your pulse to see if you are still alive and redo the experiment! When you smile or act kindly towards others to make them smile, not only do you brighten their day, but you also brighten yours.

One of my former neighbours was a 90-year-old who became a widow after 65 years of marriage. Because she was alone and heartbroken, I made a point of going to visit her regularly. Consequently, we built a deep connection, and when I used to walk into her house with my children to play cards every Sunday morning, her face would light up. The feeling we got from making her smile was powerful, and I was grateful that my children were able to sense it for themselves. They loved our card games, and they also loved spending time with her, and she became a part of our family. A few days before she died, she thanked me profoundly for my friendship and the joy we brought to her life. She said that in the 91 years she had been alive, she had never had a friend like me. I made her smile and her life better, simply by being her friend.

WHAT ACTS OF KINDNESS HAVE YOU WITNESSED THAT LEFT A LASTING IMPRESSION ON YOU?

Some human beings are truly incredible. They can love and serve beyond measure without asking for anything in return. Their reward is being instruments of love to lift and support others, which inspires me to be better every day.

My parents, especially my mum, was one of those incredible human beings. Both she and my father served others by giving food to people who were hungry. One of their greatest acts of pure kindness and generosity was towards a young man in our small town. My parents fed him daily for months on end because he had nothing. Some people thought my parents were mad, but my mum used to say something along the lines of "Who am I to judge whether he deserves our help or not," and "As long as I have it to give, I will share what I have." My mum was no pushover, either. She was a strong-willed, powerful woman, even with her beautiful, open heart. She knew the young man was grateful, so she used to give him £1 once a week to go to the local pool for a shower, warning him that if he came back smelly, she would stop feeding him – definitely not a pushover when it came to her generosity. To us, what my parents did was normal, but we did not realise how incredible they were until we grew up and saw for ourselves that not everyone was like them.

We may not be able to help others on a grand scale, feeding them daily or donating to charity, but kindness comes in many forms. We can donate our time, presence, knowledge, and wisdom, and even our blood and organs; each is of great worth. At times, we hold back as we may doubt the value of what we have to offer, but anything given with an open and loving heart is sharing positive energy. One small act of kindness from one person can transform a broken heart into a grateful one, or a bitter heart into a hopeful one, so never underestimate the power of loving acts of kindness, no matter how insignificant they may seem to you. All lives matter.

As you recall the acts of kindness you have witnessed in your life, think about how they shaped your mind and what it was about them that touched you so profoundly.

How have others served you in the past?

For most of us, it is easy to give and serve others, but to be served by others or to ask for help is not quite as easy. Parents, in particular, power through, taking care of the many aspects of family life alongside juggling their many roles outside the home and the eventualities of life. This can take its toll on our bodies, minds, and emotions, yet how often do we ask for help?

Hands up if you admit that you do not have all the answers and that we cannot manage our lives all by ourselves 100% of the time. We somehow think that asking for help is a weakness, but it is essentially a strength. It takes courage to be vulnerable enough to speak up about our struggles or admit defeat. It takes courage to accept that we are merely humans who need others to help us carry our burdens from time to time. By asking for help, we give others the opportunity to serve us, enabling them to experience the joy of giving, which, in turn, brings more joy and purpose to their lives. By denying others this opportunity, we deny them the chance to express their love through service. So, let down your guard and allow others to serve you the way you have probably served them.

By acknowledging our need for love, kindness, and compassion from each other, we begin to understand the true meaning of humility. Once we accept that we all come from the same source and that we are all of equal value, we begin to understand the very essence of life. We are soul beings, here to experience life as human beings, to love and serve each other as we go through life, but to gain the full experience of life, we have to learn to ask for help and accept help when it is offered.

I can only speak for myself here, but when I lost my parents, I also lost my sense of security. Knowing they were there somehow provided me with a safety net, a knowing that if I ever were to fall, they would be there to catch me. I believe that, in our cores, none of us actually let go of our inner-children. We grow up and have families of our own, yet we still have an innate longing to be taken care of and be loved; it is part of our humanity.

The one person to whom I run when I need support is my big sister, Marisa. I know that whenever I need some motherly love, I can go running to her. She inherited my mum's enormous heart, and even though she isn't openly affectionate, either, she always has her arms open for me. She is home to me.

As you answer this particular question, think about how others have served you. Was it something someone did, or were they simply there to love and support you through your challenges? How did you feel knowing that someone had your back?

WHO ARE THE HAPPIEST PEOPLE YOU KNOW?

Just as beauty is in the eye of the beholder, happiness is also in the eye and the mind of the beholder. This means that happiness is subject to an individual's perception. It cannot be generalised or defined for a group of people. Rather, it is a personal state of heart and mind.

In general, people tend to be happy when things are going the way they want or expect them to go and unhappy when they do not. It really is that simple. How happy we are depends on whether our projections and visions of happiness align with our realities.

For example, if your projection of happiness in this stage of your life is to be in a deep, loving relationship with your spouse or partner, spending quality time together now that your kids are grown up, and you do not have that, you will not be happy. Because your vision of a happy life did not materialise, it causes you pain, and you are not happy. The problem is not what we have or do not have; however, it is about our being so fixated on – or identified with – the original picture in our minds, that do not allow alternate possibilities to come into our lives, essentially blocking the flow of our happiness.

To remedy this, we can do one of two things: either we can change the "picture" and be open to new and exciting possibilities, or we can change ourselves and our lives to fit the picture. Either way, we need to do something. Sitting around complaining or mourning a life of which we once dreamt is like sitting back, waiting for a picture to paint itself. This will never happen, but many of us are doing just that. We eat unhealthily and hope the excess weight will just go away by itself. We laze around on the sofa, complaining we are unfit and have no energy. In essence, we expect to live happy and healthy lives without actually doing anything to make it happen.

You have probably heard this a million times, but happiness is not a destination – it is a journey of growth and progress. As we move in the direction in which we want our lives to go, we are happy simply to move forward. On the other hand, when we get stuck because obstacles are in our way, we feel frustrated and discontented. The solution? Just keep moving forward, get out of your own way, and keep yourself open to new and perhaps better things on the horizon.

So, as you think of all the happy people you know, ask yourself whether they are truly happy or whether they just align with your definition of happiness. Their definition and expectations could be very different from ours, so we cannot assume that people are happy, no matter how their lives look to us.

WHAT ACTIVITY MAKES YOU HAPPY AND LIGHTS YOU UP FROM WITHIN?

As we journey through this book and begin to recognise old thought patterns and limiting beliefs that do not serve us, we can begin to rewire our minds and start seeing a clear path ahead. This question is to help us understand what we really love to do so we can use our passions, gifts, and talents to create a more joyful existence. Another way to ask this question is, "What task or activity makes time fly for you?" No, watching TV, movies, or scrolling through social media does not count, so we have to look a little deeper. In addition, just because we are good at something does not necessarily mean that we love what we can do well.

For example, I have not worked as a hairdresser for over 20 years, but I am still good at it. Some people still stop me after all these years to say they have yet to find a hairdresser who cuts their hair as well as I did. However, I fell out of love with my work back then, which is ultimately why I quit. Just because I am good at it does not mean that I would do it again. I do not hate it – I still cut hair for my family and some of my friends because they beg me to – but just the thought of spending hours every day doing hair fills me with dread.

So, instead of focusing on what you are good at, focus on what you love doing – it may be a hobby, sport, activity, or talking to people and making them laugh. I am good at styling hair, but I love writing. I can sit and write for what feels like ten minutes, yet two hours have passed by. If I have to be somewhere on a writing day, I must set the alarm because I lose all sense of time, yet when I was in school, I hated both reading and writing. I struggled to write even a simple essay as I could not confidently string sentences together on paper, but now, all these years later, I spill my heart into my books and refuse to let any obstacles come between me and my passion. There are so many people who can write so much better than I can, but my calling to write is too loud to ignore. As long as I have a passion and love for what I do, I will keep doing what I love with joy, and I will only stop when the love runs out.

So, think about what lights you up from within and puts a bounce in your step. What excites you and fuels your energy and enthusiasm? What is *your* calling that you cannot ignore?

WHAT HAVE BEEN THE HAPPIEST MOMENTS IN YOUR ADULT LIFE THUS FAR?

We are all parents here, and the happiest moments of our lives most likely concern the arrival of our children. Even though becoming a parent is really scary and hard work and takes every ounce of our time and energy, special moments with our children are at the top of our lists of the happiest moments of our lives. We may doubt this from time to time, perhaps when we have an irate teen screaming at us for no apparent reason, but most of the time, our kids are our worlds.

My happiest memories are the precious moments I spent as a mother peacefully nursing my babies. When they looked up and smiled at me, my heart just melted. At that moment, there was a deep union of souls that was undeniably beautiful, and those memories will stay with me always. The very nature of feeding and nourishing my babies with my own milk reminded me of the miracle and beauty of life.

One mistake many of us make as parents is that we use our children as sources of happiness. Some of us have children to fill needs and desires within ourselves, so we feel loved or complete, or as outlets for all the love we have inside that we want to share. We feel needed and loved, which gives us a sense of purpose, but a lot of us (me, included) subconsciously relied on our children to make us happy.

The older our children get, the more we have to let go, and that is when we can start to lose ourselves. This may not be the case for you, but it was for me. I had become so identified with my role as a mother that I had forgotten who I was beyond being a parent. My children had filled an emptiness within me, but as they grew, the once empty space started to return, and I found myself asking, "What now?" I had essentially lost the ability to create happy moments within myself for myself.

Just because our children are growing does not mean that our purposes have been fulfilled. It is simply another chapter in the book of our lives. Our parenting duties are by no means over yet, but instead of taking care of every aspect of our children's lives, it is time for us to be examples of happiness, to guide our growing children, not just to survive to make a living in life, but to thrive and make a life. There is a whole world out there ready for us to explore, so let's enjoy it.

As you write about the happiest moments in your life, think about *why* they touched you so deeply. You will probably come to realise that these moments were not your life's greatest achievements and wins, but the beautiful, precious moments of deep connection with those you love, with nature, with life itself. We can spend our lives in search of happiness through accumulating possessions, accolades, recognition – things outside ourselves; however, it is vital that we stop to look within ourselves to see that which we already have. Through understanding what makes you happy, you begin to see that much of what you desire is already within you and around you.

WHAT DOES UNCONDITIONAL LOVE
MEAN TO YOU AS A PARENT?

Each of us would define love and happiness differently, but love between a parent and a child is unconditional. Obviously, there are exceptions to this rule, but they are rare. Unconditional love means love without conditions, a love that accepts one another for who they are, no matter what. Our children do not have to be the way we want them to be or do what we want them to do for us to love them, but is that how we felt as children? Did we have to be good and perfect to feel loved, or were we showered with love and affection even when we were out of control and misbehaving? Even though the love between a parent and a child is supposedly unconditional, is it really? I cannot answer that for you, but I do know that some of us feel unloved at times, and perhaps our children do, too.

Times have definitely changed, and most parents are openly loving and affectionate with our children, so why do our children still believe they are not loved? I used to blame my parent's lack of communication, deep conversation, and affection for me for not feeling loved as a child, so I made a point of *being* the kind of parent I wanted to have. Nevertheless, if you were to ask my kids if I loved them unconditionally, their answer would depend on their state of mind. When I ask them if they feel loved, most of the time they say they do, but there are also times when they say that they feel unloved when I tell them off, which reminds me that unconditional love is defined by each of us differently.

So, whatever way we parent, regardless of how much love and devotion we shower on them, our kids will make up their minds about whether or not we love them. Only when they are parents themselves will they really appreciate how much we love them and the enormity of the devotion we have given them; it is the circle of life. None of us really know what we have until it is gone, so why would our children be any different?

I openly talk to my children about emotions to which they roll their eyes and complain. I explain my role as their parent and tell them that even though I may make mistakes as a mother, I have to listen to my intuition and that my intention is always in their best interests, for their safety and wellbeing. I could be the parent that always says yes, but it would not be in alignment with my values. When I make decisions my children do not like, I ask them what they would do if they were me, and more often than not, they say they would make the same calls. There are also times when I am the one "ruining their lives", as they would say.

It is not our jobs as parents to make our children happy or to make life easy for them – it is our job to prepare them to be physically and emotionally self-reliant, to teach them to become strong, resilient adults, prepared for their life ahead. Showering affection and love on our children and giving them what they want to make them happy is not the only way to love them unconditionally. It is about making difficult decisions and *not* always stepping in to pick them up when they fall. It is about allowing them to learn the lessons for themselves. This, too, is an act of unconditional love in my eyes. It is easy to say yes and clean up their physical and metaphorical messes as they go so they will love us more, but is that about our need to be loved by them or about what is best for them in the long term?

The simple truth is that when we love ourselves as parents and do not seek out that love and affection from our children to fill us up, we make better parental decisions based on what is right for them instead of being desperate for their love and approval. Essentially, by doing the work on ourselves and loving ourselves more, our children's lives will be better.

Through reading your legacy, your children will come to know who you are as a person. It will help them gain a deeper understanding of their emotions growing up and make more sense of their lives, allowing them to heal. Once they know what unconditional love means to you and why you do what you do, they will be able to let go of their pasts, freeing them to move forward with greater joy.

HOW DO YOU WISH TO BE TREATED BY OTHERS?

When we are not being treated in the way we want to be treated, we feel undervalued; however, we must become aware of our behaviours and ask ourselves whether we are treating ourselves and others the way we wish to be treated. We are all very quick to judge others for their behaviours, but perhaps we need to think about how *we* show up in the world first. For me, the most important thing is being and doing *our* best, regardless of what anyone else is doing. When we judge people because their behaviours are not up to our standards, what makes our behaviours any better? As hard as it is to admit, I used to be the kind of person who judged others, forming an opinion about others without really knowing them. Funnily enough, when it happened to me, I was outraged. I am no angel, and I am still a work in progress, but now I catch myself when a judgemental thought crosses my mind. I remind myself that I do not know that person, and even if I did, I could not possibly know what is going on within their hearts and minds.

They say the road to hell is paved with good intentions, and I can see how that saying came to be. Just the other day while I was out on my daily walk, I saw a woman who lives in our little village. She is probably in her late thirties. I knew nothing about her, but the few times I have seen her, I could not decide if she were male or female. So, when I saw her on this occasion, I thought to myself, *I would love to do her hair and make-up and dress her up in something feminine*, thinking that making her look beautiful would be a lovely thing for her, but then I caught myself and said, "Stop it, Nadia! How dare you?" Who is to say she did not like herself exactly the way she was? My intentions were pure, but who was I to presume that she needed to be better? I may have had good intentions, but who did I think I was? I was judging her by her cover, exactly what I teach people *not* to do! I was grateful that I was aware enough to recognise my behaviour as well as realise that I am still a work in progress. None of us is perfect, and no matter how good our intentions are, we all fall short at times.

Being aware of our thoughts and inner-dialogue allows us to see ourselves more clearly, to bring to light the areas on which we need to work to become better, kinder people. We reap what we sow; therefore, if we judge others, we will also be judged. As you think about how you want to be treated by others, consider how you treat others – be they your spouse, partner, friends, family, or strangers – and think about the changes that need to be made within yourself. The best thing all of us can really do is to treat others as we wish to be treated, love them as we want to be loved, and hope they give us the same courtesy.

WHAT GIFTS AND TALENTS ALLOW YOU TO SHINE AND MAKE YOU FEEL TRULY ALIVE?

We talked about our gifts and talents when we were children earlier in the book, but as we grow and evolve in life, so do our gifts and talents. Things we were good at or loved doing as children may no longer be who we are now, so we have to reassess who we are and ask ourselves the right questions to understand if we are on track in life.

It is natural to presume that as we get older and wiser, our time to shine has passed, but we could not be more wrong. While there is still breath in our lungs and our hearts are still beating, we have so much to offer. We may come to a point in our lives when we feel as if we do not have the energy, but once we tap into what lights us up and allows us to glow from within, the energy of our minds, bodies, and souls will reignite, and our energies and enthusiasm will come to life.

If you have been consistently writing down the answers to each of these questions so far and using this book as it was designed to be used, then you should be ready to spark the light within you, or you may have even already lit the flame. As you get closer to the end, do not let it burn out – keep adding fuel to the flame to light the way on your journey to a new and revitalised you.

What makes your soul shine, or conversely, what makes you so mad that you feel compelled to make a change? What can you do that nobody else you know can do? As we head towards middle-age and beyond, we earn a lot more life experience than others around us, so our gifts, talents, passions, and wisdom makes us more than qualified to do what we love. The only thing to stop us is fear, but what do we have to lose? I love being middle-aged because the fears I once carried around with me are long gone. I refuse to live my life worried if I am good enough, qualified enough, or young enough to live out my dreams. If I do not go for it now, then when?

Someone I know has spoken about writing a book on health for years, and when I ask him when he is going to start, he says when he retires. He has a unique gift and has so much to offer the world, yet he says he does not have the time now, but we have to *make* the time to do what we love. If we sit for two hours every evening watching TV or scrolling through social media, that adds up to 14 hours a week, 56 hours a month, and 672 hours a year that we will never get back.

So, let's live now, use our time wisely, and start living life the way we truly desire and deserve. Deep down, we all know what our gifts, talents, and passions are but are we brave enough to step forward and shine from within as we were born to do? Are we brave enough to say yes to life? Let's not just settle for less than we desire – let's live full and meaningful lives.

How can you use your passions, gifts, talents, and experiences to lift up others?

The more you delve within yourself to share who you are in your book, the more your heart and mind will open up, and the more you will inspire your future readers. I know this is not the easiest task, but how would you feel if your middle-aged children did not live their lives out to the fullest or they settled for mediocre lives? They will turn to you and your stories at different times in their lives, especially when they feel the need for guidance and love. They may be 30-, 40-, or even 60-years-old when they take comfort in your words, so aim to inspire them by living up to your potential.

Why am I so pushy when it comes to living a full and happy life? It is to give our lives meaning and purpose, and for us to live our best lives and have reasons to get up every morning. It is the fuel we need to keep our passion for life ignited as we move forward.

Our ages have nothing to do with our abilities to live fully – it is the limits of our minds that stop us. So, as we look at our present passions, gifts, and talents, we have to tear down the blocks we have placed around us to free our spirits and tap into our souls. We are truly only limited by our imaginations.

We joke about mid-life crises, but it was very real to me and was no laughing matter. When I hit 45, my kids were growing up and no longer needed me 24/7 and panic set in. I had spent the previous 12 years in my perfect little bubble as a housewife and mother, but naively, I hadn't taken any time to think about life beyond motherhood. Here I was, lost, alone, and without plans. "*Is this it?*" I asked myself. "*Is it time to surrender and accept that the best of my life is over?*" That was when the depression crept in, but I did not know it at the time. I wanted to find a path forwards, but I had told myself so many untruths that I could not see that path. I told myself that I was too old, too behind on technology, not smart enough, not capable enough to learn new skills, and I did not have anything of worth to offer life. Once I had learned that I was telling myself untruths without evidence to back up my negative theories, I recognised what I *did* have and the gifts I had to offer the world, and I began by taking a single step.

As you consider how you can use your passions, gifts, and talents to help others, remember that your life experiences alone are of tremendous worth. You could be a lifeline for someone going through the same experiences as you who feels alone and powerless over their circumstances. You can simply be a listening ear, a hand to hold, or a shoulder on which to cry. Do not let your past pains and struggles go to waste. Instead, use your experiences to guide and lift others whichever way you can.

IF YOU HAD FAITH IN YOURSELF TO MAKE THIS WORLD A BETTER PLACE, WHAT WOULD YOU DO?

Self-belief is paramount to living a purposeful life. We do not need to know everything and be the best at what we do, but we do need to have faith in our abilities to work things out, or we would never take a single step forwards.

Regardless of our religious or spiritual beliefs, we need faith to do anything in life. Without it, we would be in a constant state of anxiety. When we drive our cars, we have faith the other drivers also know what they are doing. When we eat, we have faith the food will satisfy and nourish our bodies. When we go to sleep at night, we have faith we will wake up in the morning. These are just a few of the everyday things we do that take some level of faith on our parts so we know we can do things. All we have to do is extend our faith a little to include our purposes to bring our dreams to life.

Whether we actually reach our end goals in life is irrelevant. It is about living each and every day with joy and purpose, regardless of the outcomes. When we know our intentions are pure and what we are doing is of value, even to one other human being, then it will give our lives more meaning and purpose. There is also the chance that we will achieve our goals.

You are here, writing your story for your children and future generations because you have faith that it will be of value to them someday. The process also gives your life more meaning because of the intention behind what you are doing. Even if no one reads or values your words, which I very much doubt, at least you will have learnt a lot about yourself, and that, in itself, is a success.

As you contemplate what you could do to change the world without the possibility of failure, your true passion will come to light. It is your fears that often prevents you from attempting to make changes in the world around you. Notice the voice of your ego in your head and listen to how it manages to talk you out of stepping forward. It tries to prevent you from taking action concerning your passions and makes you fear failure, ridicule, or even being in the spotlight. It will try to discourage you in an attempt to protect you from failing but it essentially cages you in. So, exercise your faith and self-belief. Do what needs to be done to make this world better. Simply feel the fear and do it anyway because the only real failure in life is never trying.

IF YOU HAD TO WRITE A BOOK
(OTHER THAN *YOUR LEGACY*)
WHAT WOULD YOU WRITE ABOUT?

I pose this question to help open your awareness of your area of expertise. We all have unique stories to share. No two people are the same. Even identical twins who have essentially the same childhoods have different perspectives and experiences, but they are two separate hearts and minds, each with her own stories. We may tell ourselves that we are not capable of sharing our knowledge, wisdom, or experiences with others as there are people who are more professional, more knowledgeable, or more qualified than we, but they are not us, nor do they have our unique perspectives on life; therefore, they may not be able to reach everyone who needs support.

I have a heartbreaking poem hanging on my office wall, written by the daughter of a friend of mine. At the age of 22, Judith took her own life. Her words express her helplessness and the lack of power she felt in her life, and sadly, she felt as if her only escape was to take her own life. I did not know Judith personally, but her poem fuels my work and encourages me to keep going. It is a reminder of the hidden pain and suffering within others' souls that cannot be seen or heard. Above all, even though she did not see the value in her life, I sit at my desk every day, knowing full well the worth of hers.

I share Judith's poem in my book, *My Growing Heart*, as well as love lessons to help guide young people through life to help them to realise their worth and power over their lives early on. Even though Judith is not here to witness her work being put out into the world, I choose to believe that her life and death were not wasted. I know it will not reunite my friend with her daughter, but knowing that her daughter's words combined with mine may save a life one day brings her a little peace of mind.

So, no matter who you are, what you have been through, or that of which you have become a master, life has qualified you to tell your story, which can serve others in some way. You may feel as if you do not have much to offer, but if you help only one person to see the light within himself, to embrace his gifts and talents and bring joy to his life, you are living your purpose. You may have overcome a life-threatening illness, had a difficult childhood or battled with addiction in your life which has given you the experience to help others through the same challenges. You may even have the ability to make others smile or the desire to educate others on a subject about which you are passionate. Whatever your story, it is of value. Do not underestimate the power you have within you and how it can be a guiding light for others.

IF YOU KNEW YOU ONLY HAD ONE YEAR
LEFT TO LIVE, HOW WOULD YOU SPEND YOUR
REMAINING TIME?

As we near the end of this book, it is time to face the reality of our mortality. One day, we will leave this earth, but we do not know how much time we have left before then. We may have a few more decades left, or we could be gone tomorrow; tomorrow is not guaranteed.

I know this is not an easy subject to discuss, but I believe that if we keep the concept of our mortalities at the forefront of our minds, we will live happier lives. We would no longer stress over the small stuff or waste time living lives that do not bring us joy, and we would value each and every moment.

One of the biggest lessons I have learnt is that when my inner-world is joyful, then nothing outside of myself can shake me. This means that if I am at peace within my heart and mind, and I surrender my life to the universe, whatever drama or conflict there is around me cannot disturb that peace. We cannot control the world around us, but we can control how we look at and react to it.

For example, I cannot stop my body from ageing, but I can eat well, exercise, and trust my body will function at its best for me. I cannot control the outcome of my work, but I can keep writing books with loving intent, publish them, and trust they are making a difference in the lives of others. I cannot control the health and wellbeing of my children now or in the future, but I can continue to educate them, encourage them, be an example to them, and trust that the foundations I have built for them will sustain them for the rest of their lives.

As I have done the inner-work and taken this journey before you, I am already living my life with the reality of my mortality as a focal point. This may sound morbid, but the opposite is true. I live each day as if it is my last. I live each day with a peaceful heart, and I listen to the longing of my soul. If I were to die tomorrow, I would be ready. I have not left anything undone, and everyone dear to me knows how much I love them. I have written my legacy for my children that contains life lessons to assist them in their journeys. I know, for sure, that I will *not* lie on my deathbed and say, "If only I had…"

Whatever you decide to do, start. If it brings you joy, continue. If not, stop and find an alternative path. Live each day as it comes, appreciate the beauty of nature, and make time to speak, cuddle, and share beautiful moments with your children so when your time comes, you will be ready.

WHAT VALUABLE LIFE LESSONS HAVE YOU LEARNED THAT YOU WANT TO SHARE WITH YOUR LOVED ONES?

We all have core values and guiding principles by which we try to live that bring us peace of heart and mind. We may not be consciously aware of them, but they are there. Two of my primary guiding principles for life are to "Treat others as you wish to be treated", and "You reap what you sow", and I try to live by them in all that I do. I am not perfect, and I do not always hit the mark, but these principles help me navigate myself through life. Because we are so different in our ideas, it is important that we live according to our core values. Some of our core values were drummed into us by our parents, some by our religious backgrounds, some by our cultures, and some we have picked up subconsciously along the way because they just felt right to us, but it is important that we live by *our* principles and not allow ourselves to be dragged into someone else's idea of who we should be and how we should act. We have to listen to the small voices deep within our souls.

Due to my lack of self-worth and confidence at certain times in my life, I allowed other people to tell me what I was good at and what I should or should not do with my life. I was influenced by these people because I had little trust in myself and was too insecure to speak up. I settled for what was expected of me instead of looking inwards to know what was important to me, which ultimately made me unhappy. For this reason, it is vitally important to look for the answers to life's questions within rather than seek them outside of ourselves.

By sharing our life's lessons, we are not telling our children what they should or should not do. Instead, we are simply sharing our truth to guide them with the hope it will be of use to them one day. We will not always be around to protect our children, but we can provide them with the armours of knowledge and wisdom we gained in our lives. We can teach our children to live by their guiding principles to help them navigate themselves through life. It is their lives, and they have to make *their* mistakes and learn *their* life's lessons.

Even though I am 50-years-old, at times, I still want my mum. I still want her to tell me that everything will work out just fine and that I am doing a good job. I still want her words of love and wisdom. I will never be able to have that, but it brings me peace to know that even when I am gone, my children will always have my words to which to turn, and yours will, too.

Question 100

IMAGINE THAT YOU HAVE COME TO THE END OF YOUR LIFE AND ARE NOW ON YOUR DEATHBED – WHAT DO YOU WISH YOU HAD DONE DIFFERENTLY?

When I began my journey to rediscover who I was, I was asked the question, "What sentence do you want to be written on your headstone that would capture the essence of who you were in your life?" That one question hit me right to the core, and it took me two days of deep contemplation and soul searching, as well as floods of tears before I could answer. Eventually, I came up with, "She put love in our hearts and smiles on our faces". Before I was asked the question, I had no direction. I had no idea what to do or what I wanted from life other than the wellbeing of my children, but once I had answered this question, I had a destination in my heart and mind, and a wondrous new journey began. Now, I live my life with this question in my mind as a guide. Whenever I have an important decision to make, I imagine myself on my deathbed, and I ask myself how I will feel as a result of my choices. I made the decision to start writing my first book because I knew

I had to try it, or I would regret it. If I tried and failed, I would have no regrets, but by never trying…

So, I ask you the same question. It may be the hardest question of all, but your answer is essentially the key to your future and understanding your life's purpose.

When playing a game of any kind, the first thing we need to do is understand the objective of the game, or it is pointless to play, yet many of us find ourselves in the midst of the game of life, wandering aimlessly, never getting anywhere, asking "What is the point of it all?" We do not take the time to discover what we are doing or why *we* are here. We follow everyone else, thinking they have all the answers, but the answer can only be found deep within each of us. It is less about what we are *doing* to live life's purpose and more about who we are *being*.

As you imagine your life coming to an end, who do you want to be with you? Do you have any regrets? Is there something you wished you had been brave enough to do? What words have you left unsaid or deeds left undone? What will people say about you at your wake? For what do you want to be remembered?

I asked someone really close to me this last question, and she said she would want to be remembered for having a big and generous heart, which she absolutely has. She also said she would most likely be remembered for how hard she worked. This seemed to make her a little sad, but it was the wakeup call she needed to hear herself say. I am not here to tell you the purpose of your life – I do not have the answers – I simply ask the right questions to open the door to your soul, and allow you to see the love, light, joy, and potential within yourself. My wish and desire for you are that you will embrace your inner beauty and strength and realise the power within you to allow your inner light to shine. You may want to avoid facing the important questions in life and keep putting them off for fear of what you might find, but the truth is that if you do not open the doors to your hearts, minds, and souls, love and joy have no way to enter. So, as hard as this is for you, it is essential to face the truth of who you want to be and how you want to spend your precious time.

You are the author. This is the story of your life, and you choose whether it becomes a *happily ever after*.

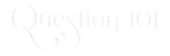

WHAT PARTING WORDS WILL YOU LEAVE YOUR FAMILY WHEN YOU LEAVE THIS EARTH THAT WILL LET THEM KNOW HOW MUCH YOU LOVE THEM?

Imagine that now is your time to go. You have lived a full and happy life, have done all you wanted to do and said everything you wanted to say. You are happy and content with the life you led, but now it is time to say your final goodbyes.

None of us knows when our times will come, so this is a rare opportunity to truly express our love for those we are leaving behind. You may think that I am being morbid, but the reality is that this day will come for all of us at some time in the future, and it is time we face that truth and use it to shape our lives instead of ignoring it. This may not be an easy feat for many of you, but believe me when I say your families will be truly grateful to read your words one day and know that they were truly loved.

My mum and I did not have the chance to say goodbye or express our love for each other, which was devastating for me. I felt cheated and angry at her death, and it took me a long time to come to terms with the fact she was gone. I know I may be asking you to open up yourself to unnecessary pain, but the gift of a goodbye for your family is worth more than anything else you could ever give them. You may not have the chance to have a final conversation, so take the opportunity to do so now. It will ultimately bring all of you peace, so this is something of immeasurable worth.

Since Mum was not the kind of person to shower her loved ones with loving sentiments, her parting words for my dad had a profound impact on his life. She had been admitted to hospital with shortness of breath and ended up being kept overnight for tests. When my dad left her that evening, she told him seven times how much she loved him – they turned out to be the last words she ever said to him because she died that night.

When we rushed to be by his side the following day, my dad said, "She must have known deep down that she wasn't going to see me again, and I should have known. She never tells me how much she loves me." Even though he never saw her alive again, her parting words of love made him smile even in the depths of his sadness, and she had left him knowing that he was truly loved.

So, you see, the parting words you share with your loved ones are priceless, and you can rest in peace, knowing that not only your words but your life mattered!

Conclusion

If you have gone through this book and completed your legacy, your life will have already changed for the better. Your eyes and hearts will have been opened, and the love and light will have broken through the doors of your soul, not only to help you as a parent but also to see the truth of who you are as a human being. Life is about continual growth. Just as we need to keep pedalling a bike to keep moving forward, you also have to keep pedalling at life to keep fulfilled and keep growing.

Regardless of the life you have led up to this point, the work you have done here has allowed you to clear the way to a bright and joyful path and open your mind to the possibilities ahead. You no longer have to fear living life as a "has-been". The time has come to reignite your flame, rediscover yourself, and live the life you want. Now is your time!

Thank you for taking this journey to leave a legacy for you and your family that will be a shining beacon in their darkest times. Your life, your time, and the love you have shared in your words is the truest expression of your love and devotion.

We began this book with wonderful words by the late Maya Angelou: "There is no greater agony than bearing an untold story inside of you." I bring this to an end by saying, "There is no greater joy than baring and sharing your soul with those who love you."

It is my wish and my blessing that your hearts will continue to shine, and your lives will be filled with an abundance of love, enthusiasm, good health, inner-peace, and joy.

With love, from my heart to yours,
Nadia
Xxx

 Nadia Wong is an author, life coach, and above all, a mother to her two teenage children. She moved from the UK to Italy in 2001 to live her dream life and start a family and has been there ever since. Due to a near-death experience in her mid-twenties, Nadia understands the true value of life and is a lifelong seeker of love, light, and truth.

Determined to share the wisdom she has gained on her life's journey, she aspires to awaken people to their inner-joy and power over their lives. Nadia's mother died suddenly when her first child was just a year old. This left her in turmoil as she desperately needed her mum at that crucial time in her life. Since then, Nadia has kept a written record of her life and that of her children, just in case she will not be with them when they need her most.

Nadia says, "I've now witnessed first-hand that none of us knows when our time to leave this earth will come, but I want to be prepared so I can leave a little part of me behind for my children."

With this declaration, *Your Life Your Legacy* was born.

Conscious Dreams
PUBLISHING

Be the author of your own destiny

Find out about our authors, events, services
and how you too can get your book journey started.

Conscious Dreams Publishing

@DreamsConscious

@consciousdreamspublishing

Daniella Blechner

www.consciousdreamspublishing.com

info@consciousdreamspublishing.com

Let's connect

Lightning Source UK Ltd.
Milton Keynes UK
UKHW022041141120
373401UK00009B/276